Love Untethered

How to live when your child dies

What people are saying about

Love Untethered

Vanessa May has written a book that can truly help all those who are grieving find deep spiritual meaning, comfort and strength. Highly recommended.
Theresa Cheung, *Sunday Times* best-selling author

Love Untethered is beautiful and gives me great hope that somehow (as a bereaved parent) we can take baby steps forward. A greater understanding of the unthinkable happening is definitely needed. Because for some of us, it did happen. The unthinkable did happen. And I take the greatest comfort from Vanessa's honesty. From the physical side of grief to the emotional side, to the behaviour of friends and the world outside – it all needs to be more out there so that the grief associated with losing a child can be better understood. I think this book will help so many.
Lucy Lyndhurst, mother of actor Archie Lyndhurst

Vanessa's book is unusual in its fusion of heart-breaking honesty and determined, resolute hope. She tells her story plainly, but never gratuitously, in an elegant style that puts the raw emotion of such a great loss centre stage. It is essential reading for the bereaved and those trying to support them. I was – and remain – deeply moved by her strength and courage.
Nancy Tucker, author of *The First Day of Spring*, *The Time In Between* and *That Was When People Started to Worry*

Love Untethered is heartfelt and beautifully written. I'm sure it will resonate with many people who have experienced losing a child.
Giles Paley-Phillips, author and host of award-nominated podcasts

I believe this is such an important work and should be a core text for counsellors. But most importantly it shares the raw essence of what it is to get through the day as a bereaved parent.

Elaine Wilkins, NHS Trainer, coaching and mentoring for health professionals

Love Untethered

How to live when your child dies

Vanessa May

Winchester, UK
Washington, USA

JOHN HUNT PUBLISHING

First published by Ayni Books, 2022
Ayni Books is an imprint of John Hunt Publishing Ltd., No. 3 East Street, Alresford
Hampshire SO24 9EE, UK
office@jhpbooks.com
www.johnhuntpublishing.com
www.ayni-books.com

For distributor details and how to order please visit the 'Ordering' section on our website.

Text copyright: Vanessa May 2021

ISBN: 978 1 80341 0487
978 1 80341 049 4 (ebook)
Library of Congress Control Number: 2021952241

A CIP catalogue record for this book is available from the British Library.

Design: Matthew Greenfield

UK: Printed and bound by CPI Group (UK) Ltd, Croydon, CR0 4YY
Printed in North America by CPI GPS partners

We operate a distinctive and ethical publishing philosophy in
all areas of our business, from our global network of authors to
production and worldwide distribution.

Contents

Introduction   1
Part One: My Story   3

Chapter 1 The Day It Happens   5
Chapter 2 The First Week of a New Life   13
Chapter 3 Disbelief and Shock   23
Chapter 4 The Funeral   30
Chapter 5 The Descent   36
Chapter 6 The Problem with Sudden Death   45
Chapter 7 The Bottom of the Sea   54
Chapter 8 Signs and Psychics   61
Chapter 9 The Inquest   74
Chapter 10 The First Holiday   79
Chapter 11 The Dark Night of the Soul   89
Chapter 12 The Unbreakable Bond   98
Chapter 13 The Abyss Again   106
Chapter 14 Survival   113

Part Two: How to Support the Grieving Process   121

Introduction: The Reality of Grief, Survival and Hope   123
Chapter 1 The Body's Response to Grief,
    Shock and Trauma   127
Chapter 2 Counselling and Alternative Therapies
    for Bereavement   137
Chapter 3 Ways to Heal   147
Chapter 4 Building Resilience and Continuing Bonds   154
Chapter 5 Who Can Help You Heal   169
Chapter 6 Going Forward Without Those We Love   178

Epilogue   182

Appendix   **187**
Reading   189
Key Organisations   191
Resources for Grief Support   194
About the Author   **198**
Acknowledgements   **200**

For Harry

Thank you for being my son

Introduction

The reality is that you will grieve forever. You will not 'get over' the loss of a loved one; you will learn to live with it. You will heal, and you will rebuild yourself around the loss you have suffered. You will be whole again but you will never be the same. Nor should you be the same nor would you want to.

Elisabeth Kübler-Ross and David Kessler, *On Grief and Grieving*

Two years ago, my son Harry died unexpectedly at the age of 24. Part One of this book is the story of how I survived the first year of living without him. I wasn't sure I could survive and often the pain of his loss was so great that I didn't want to. But I did. And so, seemingly against the odds, do most bereaved parents, their hearts forever broken.

At first, when your child dies, it feels as if all your love for them no longer has anywhere to go, that it is somehow untethered. However, the truth is, you continue to love them regardless of the fact that they are no longer physically present and, in fact, your love for them expands beyond all measure.

Throughout the first agonising year, hope would occasionally grow within me like a dandelion through a small crack in the bleak, grief-sodden earth and I would momentarily see that it might be possible to go on if I could just hold on to a reason to do so. It is still a challenge to keep focused on the light and not to slide down into the dark depths of despair. There is no choice but to go through the black tunnel of grief, and eventually, you find that hope can propel you along that tunnel towards the future. You have to move towards this light in order to stay alive, whilst at the same time carrying your child with you in your heart.

Part Two of the book is my personal guide – as a bereaved mother, nutritional therapist, wellbeing coach, and now grief coach and mentor – to withstanding such a life-changing bereavement. It provides various suggestions as to how you might support yourself through this uncharted territory, acknowledging that you're no longer the person you once were, but demonstrating that you can build a life around your loss, eventually. Not the life you envisaged but a different one, where you honour your child and make them proud of you as you live on without them. It is a life sustained by your untethered love.

Part One
My Story

Chapter 1

The Day It Happens

The night he died, the moon asked 'how much of her life will change by morning?' and the wind whispered: 'everything the sunlight touches'.

Grief to Glorious Unfolding

There is nothing about this particular Saturday to indicate that something is going to happen to transform my life beyond anything I could possibly imagine. Nothing to suggest that, by tomorrow evening, I will be a changed person, having walked through a door to an entirely different life. That door will divide my life into before and after, slamming behind me with breathtaking callousness and ensuring that I can never return to the world I once inhabited. But, for now, I believe this Saturday to be a perfectly ordinary day and I live it without any knowledge of the catastrophic event that will occur at around two o'clock.

During the morning I see two clients. Harry comes into my mind whilst I see one of them as he's a young man of a similar age, and I remind myself to text Harry later in the afternoon. I hope he will be sleeping as he finished his fourth 12-hour night shift this morning. I will ask him if he wants to come over for something to eat on Monday evening.

During the afternoon, I happen to start watching, with no inkling yet of the irony, the film *Manchester by the Sea*. Around 4 p.m. I text Harry: 'Everything okay? x'. He doesn't reply. He's not been great about replying to texts since he moved out but maybe he's still sleeping. I remind myself that he's a grown man and doesn't need his mum bothering him all the time.

I wake on Sunday morning, still oblivious to what took place yesterday. No suspicion, no niggling feeling, no intuition that something is wrong. I do start to worry as the day goes on, though only as I might normally do. I watch the rest of *Manchester by the Sea* curled up on the sofa in my pyjamas. I think about the grief the characters experience and wonder how I will cope when my mum dies, something I've been dreading for years. Harry still hasn't replied. Perhaps he was out late last night and is still asleep. I don't want to nag him; I'll leave it just a bit longer...

By mid-afternoon, my concern is steadily escalating. I say to Anthony that I still haven't heard from Harry and that 'he could be lying dead for all we know'. This isn't the first time I've said this. I've had this seemingly irrational fear since he moved out to a room in a flat with four strangers. I don't know why I've been having this quiet, ongoing dread and I try very hard to dismiss it.

I ring Harry and it goes to voicemail. I wait a bit and try again. I leave a message. It's now around 4 p.m. and I'm going against my instincts, telling myself that he'll be fine. At 5 p.m. Anthony says he'll go around to his flat, just to set my mind at rest.

As soon as Anthony goes, something in me begins to shift on a physical level. I start to feel nauseous and my heart begins to race. Still, I override my mountingly strong instincts, now taking this tangible form, and I tell myself to stop it, to stop worrying, Harry will be okay. My phone rings, it's Anthony. He says he's outside and that he can't see any lights on in Harry's room. My stomach flips over. He says Harry's probably out or asleep and he doesn't want to annoy him by letting himself into his room. I'm panicking now: 'Go in! It doesn't matter – he'll understand that we're just worried.'

He says he'll ring back when he's inside. My world is now turning on its axis and I know; I know in my heart and on some deep primal level that – what? – I can't quite go there, it's too much. I wait for Anthony's call. It doesn't come. I think I might be sick. I ring him, he picks up, he's sobbing. 'What?!' I scream. 'I think he's dead!' he cries. My brain becomes confused, it won't compute. This information isn't true. I can't allow this to be true, I won't accept it! My heart is pounding out of my chest, I'm shaking uncontrollably and I'm freefalling now, spinning out of control. I have to get to my boy *now* – it might not be too late – I could save him! If anyone can, it would surely be me, I gave birth to him, he's my boy.

'NO NO NO God, please no!!'

I'm talking to myself out loud, I'm hysterical. Then I freeze. I actually pinch myself to see if I can feel something because this has to be the worst nightmare ever and it definitely, most definitely, cannot be real.

How will I get to him? Anthony took the car. I can't think straight because my brain seems to have stopped working properly. My daughter, Lily, on her way home from seeing her boyfriend Tom, can order me an Uber on her account – yes, good idea. As I ring, I think I had better not say what's happened to her brother yet but I realise then that actually, I can hardly speak. I really am hysterical and I'm not forming proper sentences. She is calm in the face of my panic, asking for Harry's address, which I just can't recall – it's somehow slipped out of my mind. I would know how to get there but have inexplicably forgotten the name of the road. Everything's slipping and unreal, which is why it really can't possibly be true and is just an unfathomably horrifying dream. But still, I tell Lily to get to Harry's flat and I'll meet her there. I realise somewhere inside that this will be life-changing for her and I've messed up how she should find out, but I've completely lost my rational mind. I have to get to Harry – I put on my coat over my pyjamas, grab my phone and keys and go to one of our neighbours.

I ask through my simmering hysteria if she can take me to

Harry's because I think he's dead. I say 'think' but I actually know. I don't want to accept it, though, so I stick to 'think'. She goes upstairs and I wonder if perhaps she hasn't grasped the urgency of the situation, so I cry: 'PLEASE HURRY UP!' Her husband comes to the doorway and, towering over me, shouts with an astounding burst of anger: 'Alright, she's coming, calm down!' I find this so incredibly shocking; it winds me, exacerbating my already very considerable distress.

Eventually, we get in the car – texts are coming through from Lily but I don't have my glasses to read them. It's very cold, the windows are frosty and time seems to stretch to make this the longest journey of my life. Everything's slowed down, like a nightmare where you feel unable to move with the urgency you need to. I am completely and utterly beside myself. I scream to go through lights that are turning from amber to red and to drive faster. I feel so sick, so shaky, so very unlike myself. My stomach somersaults at the sight of the ambulance as we pull up. I ask my neighbour if she will wait downstairs for Lily to arrive. I run up the stairs – I just need to be with my boy, please God make it alright somehow, I'll do anything, anything...

Anthony meets me at the door crying, and I run into the room screaming.

'NO NO NO NO NO!'

I drop to my knees and make some kind of sound that comes from my gut or the depths of my very soul. There's my precious boy on his bed so clearly *gone*. I sit next to him, he's stiff and he's very, very cold. I must warm him up. I put my body over him, I pull up the duvet but I know, I know he's gone. His eyes are three-quarters closed and he has a slightly surprised expression on his face. One hand is on his chest. This is not right, this is so very, very wrong.

The two paramedics stand in the middle of the room – one woman, quite young, looks embarrassed by this outpouring of such extreme emotion. Neither show any sign of humanity or say anything to us. I'd like them to go but vaguely suppose they can't for some reason. A man comes to the door with a disingenuous smile – I don't know who he is but I find myself smiling back. Has he come to help, to tell us something? It turns out he's one of the other occupants of the flat – why is he intruding? Is he loving this bit of drama in his otherwise dull life? Why are people simply not grasping the full extent of this dreadful tragedy?

Lily – we must tell her. Is she here yet? I go downstairs to see. She is there with our neighbour. She is understandably distressed but she doesn't want to come upstairs. It turns out this 'flatmate' has already told her that her brother's dead. Part of me freezes and shuts down with incomprehensible disbelief at the whole situation.

Anthony and I wait in Harry's room for the police to arrive. They take ages. Good, I think, I need this time with Harry, it's the last time I'll ever get the chance to be with him, so I had better make the most of it. I feel so terribly sick and I shake from head to foot – I realise that I'm in shock.

I look around me. Harry was so excited to make his first place away from home exactly the way he wanted. His large desk with a big screen for playing games and watching Netflix, his record player, giant speakers, his music equipment, guitars and the sofa his grandma had only given him a couple of weeks ago. The fairy lights around the windows are on. If he died yesterday then these have been on all this time. It feels utterly heartbreaking, like a life has been interrupted mid-flow. Which, of course, it has.

Eventually two police officers arrive and take us into the communal kitchen. I haven't drunk anything for ages but I keep going to the loo – interesting, I find myself thinking, how your metabolism must speed up when you're in extreme shock. So far, no one has even offered to make us a cup of tea. The policeman observes that I'm very pale and shaking and gets a chair for me. Some kindness at last. The policewoman talks to me about how she has lost two siblings. I say I'm concerned about my daughter. The policewoman says, speaking from her own experience, that Lily will have to step up now. It seems a very heavy burden to place on Lily's slight shoulders; she's barely more than a teenager. I realise with immense sadness that she's become my only child.

Soon these police officers go and two more arrive, who are higher-ranking but not so blessed with empathy. They say they have to search Harry's room to rule out foul play. They shut Harry's door whilst we remain in the kitchen. It's all completely surreal and I don't seem to be able to fully grasp what has happened, it's all just out of reach. I become slightly obsessed with my physical symptoms – the shaking, racing heart, catching my breath, feeling faint, like I'm not really in my body, and so very nauseous. Lily decides not to see Harry, and I'm grateful that my neighbour has remained downstairs with her so that she's not on her own. I feel bad for dragging the neighbour into our family tragedy. Before she eventually goes home, I tell her I always feared I wouldn't have Harry for long, and that my life is over now it's been so brutally severed by his death. It's just unimaginable that I will be able to continue to live.

Finally, the police come out of the room and ask the other occupants of the flat when they last saw Harry and how did he seem. The one we have encountered earlier can't wait to tell them helpfully that Harry had been looking rather gaunt the last time he saw him. I feel angry as I overhear this. If he thought Harry didn't look well, did he actually ask him whether he was alright, if there was anything he could do, anyone he could call? I want to scream at him 'Why didn't you do something? You might have saved his life!'

The policemen tell us that it doesn't look like foul play and that we now have to wait for the funeral directors to collect

Harry's body. I feel a jolt of terror that murder has even been considered a possibility. It's all so bewildering and we stand by helplessly as other people, who don't know or care about our son, take control of the situation. We are told there will be a postmortem and inquest as the cause of death is 'unexplained'.

I find their lack of sensitivity surprising: we are parents who have lost their son, visibly in a great deal of distress. I look around Harry's room with its empty pizza box, takeaway coffee cup, half-eaten croissant, clothes all over the floor, plus of course I'm in my pyjamas, and I feel we are rather judged. I will find in the weeks to come that people's less than benevolent reactions to my exposed vulnerability, whether the police, the paramedics, the neighbour's husband, or others I will later come across, add unnecessary salt to my wound. As if what I'm already experiencing isn't appalling enough...

Several hours later, when Harry's body has been taken away, we get a bin bag and make a rather frenzied attempt to tidy his room. I'm not sure why we do this. Perhaps we feel this is the only thing we can do for him now. Finally, Anthony, Lily and I – our diminished family of three – head home. The worst has happened. Our world is now tilting at a precarious angle. Everything has irrevocably changed and I have a strong sense, in amongst the overriding physical symptoms of shock, that it will be difficult for me to survive this, the loss of my child, my firstborn, my adored boy.

The Night After

No one ever told me that grief felt so like fear.
CS Lewis, *A Grief Observed*

I lie in bed with my heart beating out of my chest, adrenaline coursing through my body, and a gnawing in my stomach. I shake but I don't cry. Anthony sleeps, seemingly peacefully, next to me. I start to think about how I will tell my mum and break her heart. I think of all the other people I will have to tell and how I need to cancel all my clients for the next week. I may as well get up...

So, at 3 a.m. I cancel all my forthcoming appointments and put a notice on my website saying I won't be taking on any new clients due to bereavement. 'Bereavement' – as I type the word it feels completely unbelievable that I am having to write this. Harry had only recently completed my website. He did everything technical for me. I wonder numbly about how I will manage without him – how? I will now have to live without the best hugs in the world, his boundless love, his sense of humour, his kindness, his wonderful company. It's unfathomable. I will never again have to nag him about eating vegetables or tidying his room. I might have imagined once it would be a relief not to do so, but now, I'd give anything, literally anything, to be just an ordinary mum concerned with ordinary worries – rather than one who is so utterly destroyed and heartbroken by the death of her child.

Because I recognise that my body is displaying symptoms of extreme shock which don't seem to be abating, the nutritional therapist in me kicks in and I decide to order some supplements. I think of what I normally suggest to other people for calming the nervous system, supporting the adrenals and to help with sleep. I even helpfully recall a homeopathic remedy for grief. I place a big order.

Chapter 2

The First Week of a New Life

An unimaginable, indescribable loss has taken place. It has inflicted a wound so deep that numbness and excruciating pain are the material of which it is made...Your life continues, but you are not sure why...No one can give you words to make you feel better; there are none. You will survive, though you may not be sure how or even if you want to.

Elisabeth Kübler-Ross and David Kessler, *On Grief and Grieving*

Anthony and Lily are up. They have slept. I don't understand how this is possible but I am glad for them. They also eat. I can't. I seem physically unable to chew or swallow and I know I will be sick if I do. The shaking, the racing heart and the nausea continue and everything feels so unreal. I don't feel as if I'm properly in my body. We start to make phone calls. I don't remember much about these but I do remember telling one of Harry's godmothers, and she is distraught. I keep saying I am sorry over and over as she cries in disbelief at what I have told her. I speak to one of Harry's friends who he worked with – he is inconsolable too – no one can believe it.

I vaguely think I shouldn't drive but I have to go to Mum's. I know this is one of the worst things I will have to do and for some reason I feel I should do it alone, that only I can impart the dreadful information.

I sit my mum down and I ask her to prepare herself for some very bad news. She is shocked when I tell her and doesn't really take it in at this stage. As I'm talking, I find my brain has frozen and I repeat the word 'he' over and over, like a stuck record. Mum says, 'Let's get you home,' and I drive for what will be the last time in many weeks.

13

Once home, I break down. I collapse and wail. Shock is incredible in that it protects you from being in excruciating emotional anguish for too long at a time, but when it hits, I feel it will kill me. Later there will be no protection, but for now, I come out of the pain for periods of time and continue to inform people that Harry is dead. He's actually dead, no longer here, gone, left us. His precious short life is over. Sometimes I connect with the astonishing truth of this and sometimes I don't.

Anthony, Lily, Mum and I sit in the living room drinking tea and we all realise that we don't know what we are meant to do. There has to be a postmortem so we have no idea when we can arrange a funeral. There are no instructions for this, no one to advise us of what to do in such a situation – we feel lost and adrift. We thought our lives were going one way, but it seems we have taken a very unexpected fork in the road. We've so many people to tell and I desperately need to get the delivering of the news over with. I am hanging on by a very thin and fraying thread but somehow time slips by and it's the afternoon.

A friend of Harry's rings Anthony and says they want to raise money for a bench in Harry's name. A group of Harry's old friends from his teenage years have met up and a group of his current friends have done so too. The two groups are in touch with each other and want to know if some of them can come over. They want to help and support us. We say maybe later in the week, that we are in too much shock right now. We tell them how touched Harry would be. Soon the GoFundMe page for the bench appears online and we are moved by the tribute his friends write. The donation goal is exceeded within four hours. We are surrounded by love and we appreciate it. We are pleased Harry meant so much to others and not just to us.

Lily tells us about her good Samaritans. As she took my hysterical call, she got off the bus she was on, not knowing how she could get to Harry's flat. She knew where he lived but didn't have his actual address and, in my distress, I hadn't been able to remember it. A couple on the bus had overheard her talking to me on the phone and, guessing that something bad had happened, offered to drive her to wherever she needed to go. She walked with these total strangers to their home where they got in their car and took her to Harry's flat. An extraordinary act of kindness.

The coroner's office call. We can choose a funeral director as the postmortem has been done and the body can be released. Now we have something to do. But we are not ourselves and time is not as it was. We feel slowed down, have difficulty making decisions. I avoid thinking about how my boy has been on a cold slab, cut up, dissected like a piece of meat. It feels as if I'm in my own personal horror story, yet there is also a certain numbness. Shock, denial and disbelief protect me – to some extent anyway.

I continue to find it impossible to sleep and the shaking and racing heart continue. On the second day of this new life, I am still unable to eat. Anthony finds a couple of funeral directors and we go to visit them. At the first one, the woman is kind as I cry, and she gives me a booklet of poems for funerals. Decisions have to be made and I have no experience of any of this. It's all so unfamiliar and unexpected. She pulls back a curtain and shows us some coffins lined up on the wall – I am horrified. How can I put my adored son in a wooden box – that's for old people! Beyond exhausted, I say to Anthony, 'Let's just go with them, they seem nice,' but he says we have an appointment with the second funeral director and should keep it.

I just don't want to go through everything again, I am so drained, but the second funeral directors tell us we can have a wicker coffin and they have a florist who can weave flowers through and I think, *Yes, how lovely.* I am concerned about Harry's hair, I tell them. He had been wearing a beanie hat when he died and his hair could do with a wash. The funeral director tells me he can wash it for us. They show us beautiful glass artwork with some blue waves that you can put some of the ashes in – 'What a fantastic idea,' I say. However, during the night as I lie awake, I wonder what I was thinking – Harry didn't really like the sea. I imagine him saying 'Mum, why have you trapped me in this wave, I hate the sea!' I am not myself and I think I'm probably not to be trusted to make decisions.

The rest of the first week goes by. Friends bring food and I try to eat, which seems easier if someone else has made it, but I don't manage much. We go back to Harry's flat and realise we will have to start to clear it soon as his lease runs out at the end of the month. We go from tears of heartbreak to numb shock and the latter at least allows us to be practical. I water the two big plants that were our Christmas present and which seem now to be dying. I find the book I gave him – *How Not to Kill Your House Plants*...

People constantly ring or text to check on us. Jack and Jessie, Anthony's older children, come to see us. They are devastated by the news and are deeply affected by Harry's passing. Being a generation older than Harry and Lily, they took on the role of older siblings to them with great love and generosity, always. As we sit around the table having lunch, none of us can believe we're doing so without Harry. We hug and cry together, sharing our love as if it might somehow bring our Harry back.

Harry's friends and one of my closest friends come over. It consoles us to see how affected people are, to see they cared and that Harry made an impact on their lives. We hear that the dad of an ex-girlfriend cried for several hours when he heard the news. Other people's love for Harry and for us is a comfort but I am now so unbelievably, bone-crushingly tired. I am taking every supplement, herbal and homeopathic remedy I have ever come across through my work but nothing seems to touch the sides in the extremity of a situation like this.

I get into bed at night, try to read a book in order to wind my brain down but remain on the same page for many days. I then switch off the light and see the image of Harry lying dead, rigid and icy cold on his bed. I get horribly unpleasant adrenaline surges. I feel overwhelming fear and panic. After several hours I might drift off but then I wake with a jolt, the adrenaline kicking in again. I seem to have several hours wide awake between around 2.30 and 6 a.m. every morning and, if I'm lucky, I may nod off for an hour until 7 a.m. I realise I must be extremely traumatised.

Arranging the Funeral

A wife who loses a husband is called a widow.
A husband who loses a wife is called a widower.
A child who loses his parents is called an orphan.
There is no word for a parent who loses a child.
That's how awful the loss is.
Jay Neugeboren, *An Orphan's Tale*

You wouldn't plan a wedding in a couple of weeks, yet this is standard for a funeral. I am now very, very sleep-deprived and running on empty. However, I feel clear about what I want for Harry – a church service followed by a brief service at the crematorium. I want songs that Harry loved and lots of projected photos. A service that reflects who he was as much as possible, an incredible, irreplaceable young man. Anthony and Lily agree but some friends question why we want a church service when none of us go to church. 'Is it what he would want?', they ask doubtfully. But I remember attending two very moving services held at our local church – for the husband and five-year-old son of a friend I met at a pregnancy yoga class, and I know with certainty that this is where we should hold Harry's funeral.

The vicar comes to see us. He accepts that Harry was not religious and totally gets what we want. We concede to a hymn as he says this helps to give people a voice: we settle on 'Morning Has Broken'. He says to leave the crematorium service to him. He delegates the sending through of the music and the photos for the church service to Lily, seeming to understand that she needs a part in all of this. I have complete trust in him and feel he's a safe pair of hands. He seems genuinely compassionate and I later find out he has children of a similar age to Harry and Lily. He suggests we prepare for a lot of people, more than we might anticipate, and he warns me that the crematorium will be the hardest part as that will be where we have to finally say goodbye to Harry.

Anthony, Lily and I are very united in our grief at this stage, uniquely connected by our family tragedy. We support each other as best we can. I write lists of all that has to be done. Planning and being organised is what I do well. The funeral arrangements keep me busy but I am now obsessed with sleep – both serve to keep me away from the pain. Cards and flowers keep on coming and I feel so touched by the kindness towards us. Our shocking loss has even affected people we don't really know – a woman I sat next to at someone's birthday lunch, the parents of a boy with whom Harry went to university – and everyone who knew Harry writes such lovely things about him. The love flowing towards us and Harry is wonderful, and I feel a sense of incredulity that something this monumental has happened to our family. Why us? The contrast between the warm and comforting outpouring of love and the horrifying reality of our loss is confusing. How can it be true that Harry has actually gone? I want him to be here to appreciate how much everyone cares, how special he is, how he has touched people's lives with his kind, loving and generous nature.

We decide on an Order of Service programme that will have

lots of photos and our eulogies in it. Looking through old photos is bittersweet. As a teenager and adult, Harry hated having his photo taken, preferring to take pictures of others, so there are few good ones of recent years that we can find. This upsets me and I feel quite cross with him. Lily takes over the layout of the Order of Service which will eventually and understandably prove stressful, the enormity of taking on this task to honour her big brother completely overwhelming her. She's just 20 and it's so very sad that her young life is now marred by such tragic adversity. But her boyfriend Tom supports her and they do Harry proud with the programme they produce.

We leave the organising of the wake to Harry's friends. This will be their part of the day and one I already suspect I won't be able to attend. We ask his closest friends if they will deliver a tribute at the funeral and we ask an ex-girlfriend, together with his closest female friend, to read a poem. The boys will also carry his coffin. We want to involve everyone who loved him.

People start to tell me how strong I am. I wonder in unutterable disbelief how they can possibly think this when I am so very clearly falling apart. Their lack of understanding regarding this throws me off balance and isolates me because it appears I'm the only one who comprehends that 'strong' is not a word to accurately describe me right now. I have never felt less strong in my entire life. In fact, I really can't understand how I am still standing, still actually alive. Why have I not died of a broken heart yet? I have a foreboding sense that, even though I am most definitely in a certain kind of hell, the worst is yet to come. I worry about the toll that being constantly on high alert, together with lack of sleep, will have on my body. This distracts me from what's going on at a deeper level – the raw gaping wound in my psyche.

I just can't properly comprehend that Harry has left us. He just wouldn't do this, it's so unlike him. Surely there was so much more for him to do in life? It makes no sense that he is suddenly just gone. One afternoon, as I try unsuccessfully to have a nap, I have a sort of vision, in my half-waking state, of his arm with a tattoo crudely etched in blood which says: 'Forgive me.' It is very vivid, and I wonder if it's a message from him.

There is one person I really want to see at this point, the only person I know who will truly understand, the only person I know who shares this experience, and that's the friend who lost her five-year-old son ten years ago and her husband two years prior to that. Her losses had a profound effect on me and I felt such enormous sadness for her. I have often wondered how she survived and thought that I definitely wouldn't if it happened to me. I had imagined her pain, but now I feel it for myself.

When she visits me, she talks to me about the nature of this particular grief but also gives me a glimmer of hope by telling me she sometimes feels her son with her and that the pain will eventually lessen in its intensity. I am so terribly tired; I can hardly string a sentence together. I lie down on the sofa and she covers me with a blanket. She gives me a hug, one bereaved mother to another, and quietly leaves.

Anthony and I become detectives and obsess over piecing together how Harry died, knowing that the inquest is likely to be months away. I fret over how, despite buying every kitchen utensil available when he first moved out, Harry didn't eat well and mainly lived on ready meals and takeaways. My job means I know very well how a poor diet can have considerable health consequences and Harry was naturally very thin, regardless of how much he ate. He suffered from allergies, crippling migraines and insomnia – all of which had been getting steadily worse. I think, in hindsight, that his body must have been slowly declining. I find that I now understand from personal experience how distressing and debilitating sleep deprivation is and I think of him as I lie awake, knowing now what it's like. His twice-monthly sets of night shifts at the media company he worked for had most certainly been taking their toll. As someone who already had problems with insomnia, they made the issue so much worse and he would really struggle to sleep. Night shifts are known to be disruptive to the circadian rhythm and have negative health implications. This, and the potentially very serious effects of chronic sleep deprivation, will, we increasingly come to believe, have been contributory factors in his death.

Other facts come to light – Harry felt unwell on that last set of night shifts but couldn't get anyone to cover him, so he went in. As he left work on the morning of the day he died, he told a colleague he didn't feel well. What kind of unwell, we wonder, with the frustration of probably never knowing. Was it a migraine, a virus, what? I feel so utterly heartbroken at being deprived, as his mum, of looking after him, making him better, keeping him alive, preventing him from dying. We look at his bank accounts, Netflix, Uber and Deliveroo accounts for clues. We discover that in the days prior to his death, he was ordering takeaways and watching films during the hours when he should have been asleep, but must have been unable to…

I think about the half-eaten croissant we found in his room. Harry must have stopped off after finishing work to buy it for breakfast, along with a coffee. Did he begin to eat it on the Tube and then thought he'd save the rest for when he got back to his flat? Did feeling unwell mean he'd lost his appetite? I struggle to make sense of the fact that a few hours after buying that croissant he was dead. He saved the croissant. He clearly didn't expect to die. His death must have felt so unanticipated to him, as well as to us. I wish now I'd kept it – the last thing he ate.

The clothes he was wearing when he died are returned. Two

T-shirts, two thick sweatshirts, a beanie hat, jogging bottoms. He had been under the duvet when we found him. Just how cold was he? Did he have a fever, die of hypothermia? Why does the pathologist or coroner not ask us for any information? We would like to humanise our son and tell them that he was a wonderful person. It is all so horribly distressing.

We conclude there may have been many contributory factors, along with the likelihood he self-medicated with something to help him sleep and for the pain of a migraine and/or a possible virus. Maybe this was the final straw for his stressed and weakened body. If only he'd told us he didn't feel well, if only I'd rung him, if only, if only, if only...

Chapter 3

Disbelief and Shock

I loved the boy with the utmost love of which my soul is capable, and he is taken from me – yet in the agony of my spirit in surrendering such a treasure I feel a thousand times richer than if I had never possessed it.
William Wordsworth

In the limbo between his death and his funeral, I try to focus on how lucky I was that I had a truly remarkable relationship with Harry, that we were securely bonded from the start and that, despite the obligatory difficult teenage years, we remained so. He had such an enormous capacity for love. There was nothing unfinished or unsaid between us, and for that I am grateful. I think of the last time I saw him. How I took him lunch with extra salad and fruit and felt so happy and excited to see him, as I always did when I visited him, during those five short months he had lived on his own. We laughed and chatted; he made me feel so loved, always, but particularly as he became an adult. I'm pleased that I actually appreciated this at the time and not just retrospectively.

But inexplicably over the last year or so, I worried about him more than I ever had before, as if I had some sense that I wouldn't have him much longer. When he was younger, he could be fearless. He would climb to the top of the tallest tree and I seemed to know he wouldn't fall, as if he was somehow protected. I worried later, in the usual way of mothers with teenagers or young adults, about him being out late at night, getting very drunk or getting stabbed. But latterly, whilst he was still at home and then in his flat for the last few months of his life, I became especially anxious about him for no newly justifiable reason. Did I know on some level that I would lose him and that it would be soon?

Given this apparent foresight, I don't understand why I didn't sense anything at the time he actually died. How could I not know? I feel like this is some kind of failure on my part as a mother. My maternal instincts found wanting at this most crucial moment, as I spent what I thought was a normal Saturday afternoon in complete ignorance that my son was passing away.

I recall how Harry had met an American rapper called Lil Peep on a trip to Berlin and told me how lovely he was to him. I remember being quite judgemental about this heavily tattooed musician, but Harry was very eclectic in his music tastes. Later, Lil Peep died from an accidental drugs overdose and, because he had met him, Harry was quite affected by this. I remember going into his bedroom when he was playing a Lil Peep song called 'Tell My Mom I'm Sorry'. Now tragically this young man I saw on the screen was dead. I started to get upset, saying, 'Please promise me you'll never do anything stupid, Harry... I couldn't go on if anything happened to you, I honestly wouldn't survive.' Harry reassured me that nothing was going to happen to him and gave me a hug, but I strongly recall the anguish I felt for this young life lost and the poor mother who had lost her son. Now Harry is the young life lost and I am the mother who has lost her son.

It's all so disorientating. We continue to oscillate between desperate gut-wrenching despair and doing what we have to do on a practical level to prepare for the funeral. We go to see Harry's body at the funeral directors and take some things to put in our very tall boy's extra-long coffin: the last album he had been playing, Lily's crystal for protection, his favourite 'Relax' teabags, a guitar plectrum, a beanie hat, a camera film container filled with jelly beans, a pair of his pink sunglasses, Lily's Magician tarot card and a necklace, plus cards and notes from Anthony, Mum and me.

My note ends:

> I have never loved anyone more than I loved and love you
> – my heart was always so full of love for you and that will
> never ever end. You were and will remain my world until I
> join you. But I will try to live for you, Dad, Lily and Grandma
> – if you can show me you are around me, please do.
>   I was lucky to love you and to have been so loved by you
> – a love that was pure, light and golden between us. Let your
> soul and spirit be at peace, darling – it's what I want for you
> – and just continue to love and be with me in whatever way
> that can be now.

But I wish I hadn't seen him. He has been embalmed and he
doesn't look like him. A waxwork, his face appears weirdly
stretched and his torso seems to have some kind of padding
or bandage under his shirt. I try not to think too much about
whether this is due to the dissection of his body during the
postmortem, aware that this is a possibility no mother should
have to consider. Everything that's happened is so utterly
horrendous but we're becoming strangely accustomed to
dealing with yet more than we ever in our worst nightmare
thought we'd have to endure. I am grateful Harry has clean hair
and I appreciate the funeral director has tried to make it look
like it does in the photograph we provided. Anthony finds it
helpful to be with Harry and goes back again a few days later.
We are finding different ways to deal with our loss.

I am now starting to read books on grief and learning that it
is normal for the two members of a couple to grieve in different
ways. My thirst for any book on grief, specifically the grief of
losing your child, will continue for many months and reading
is one of the few things that helps me. As well as finding some

small crumbs of comfort in reading about the experiences of other bereaved mothers, I am desperate to make some sense of what I'm going through, to understand a way to navigate through the pain, to understand when it might end, if in fact, it does end.

I read that marriages can disintegrate when your child dies but this doesn't seem to be the case for us. Perhaps being in a long marriage is an advantage as Anthony and I know each other so well and can anticipate and respect our differences. Despite being heartbroken and traumatised himself, Anthony hasn't fallen apart in the same way as I have and I appreciate how he is trying to be strong for me. When he receives news that he's got a job in a few months' time that may take him away from home for several days, I crumble. It frightens me how much I now rely on him. I have never really been dependent on him in all the time we've been together but now I find I very much need him for my survival. I wonder if, in turn, it helps his survival to be needed. I think it probably does and, for now, these appear to be our new roles within the marriage. And on the whole, we are finding that our grief brings us closer together because only we share the experience of what it feels like to lose our wonderful son.

Everyone offers to help: 'If there's anything I can do please just ask,' they say. This is lovely, but the best help comes when people just take over and get on with something, like bringing a meal or checking on my mum. Everyone is so kind, and I feel proud of Harry's friends in particular for really stepping up for us. They message Lily, as do our family friends who check that she isn't getting overlooked, sending her thoughtful texts and little gifts. Although Lily and Tom haven't been together all that long, he is being so supportive of her, as are his family. Lily stays with them most weekends, taking a break from witnessing the brokenness of her parents, needing some normality around her.

Due to my exhaustion, I feel drained by spending time with

people, but hearing their stories about Harry lifts us. We already know about his kindness, his sensitivity, his talent and creativity and how funny he is. However, things we didn't really know about him come to light. That he could enjoy a good gossip (I can't imagine where he got that from), that girls loved him (which we sort of knew), that he could be the life and soul and get a party or gathering going with his much-respected music choices, that he could be a peacemaker and break up fights, that he had composed over 80 songs, that it wasn't just us that loved him.

I write my eulogy. I know I won't be up to reading it so I ask a close friend if she will read it for me. In hindsight, this responsibility must have been daunting for her, though she does both me and Harry proud. I write it with urgency and from the heart and send it to two other good friends to proofread for me.

My lovely Harry

Harry was the most amazing son I could ever have wished for and when I gave birth to him 24 years ago my life changed for ever and for the better.

I was so fortunate to have such a strong bond with my beautiful blond boy and I am comforted by being secure in the knowledge that he loved me very much and I, of course, unconditionally loved and adored him.

Life wasn't always easy – Harry was sometimes a rebel and refused to conform – but I often secretly admired his spirit and strength of character.

Harry loved his family, his friends, his cats, his music, films, photography, games and clothes – so many clothes! He built all my websites from the age of 14 and never hesitated to help me with anything technological. He was talented and creative but above all he had a very big heart.

He would have hated to be the centre of attention today but would have been so incredibly touched by the love everyone has for him and to see just how much he meant to you all. He would be proud to see how his close friends have stepped up to support his family.

Harry was fiercely loyal, incredibly generous, very funny, modest, charming, affectionate and so protective of his Mum. He would be devastated to see me so broken hearted.

We are a close family. There was no doubt about his love for his Dad and their shared humour, his care for Lily and for his Grandma. He also had a lovely relationship with Jack and Jessie. We were fortunate that we have the memory of a very happy last Christmas with him. When there was a possibility of him working over Christmas he said: 'Don't worry Mum, I'll just tell them my Mum will cry if I'm not there'.

And he still loved a family holiday – the four of us went away together at least once a year up until last year and I am so thankful for the very happy memories I will always have of these special times.

Just before he died, Harry asked me to look over his CV and covering letter as he was applying for a promotion. When I said what would he say if asked what qualities he would bring to this managerial role he replied he felt that he was fair, good at explaining things and that people liked him. I told him how very proud I was of the man he had become.

Once Harry left home last summer, I used to really look forward to visiting him and my heart would feel so full of love. The last time I saw him was the week before he passed away. I took him some food and we had lunch together. He was always such great company and made me laugh so much. He gave me plenty of hugs, as always, and as I left, told me he loved me. I feel so very blessed to have had him in my life for those precious 24 years.

Lily also wants to write a eulogy and read it herself. I admire her greatly for wanting to do this. Anthony will read a poem. They are both braver than me. But I can organise. I tell everyone when and where the funeral is. I get a group together to bake cakes for after the church service. I specify the flowers I want. I decide on the order of the church service. I choose the photos. I need to control something in these very out-of-control times.

Deciding upon the music for the service is particularly painful. We decide on a mix of songs we used to listen to in the car on the way to school or on holidays, as well as music that Harry and Lily shared between them. We then select one of Harry's own compositions to be played during the prayer/ reflection part of the service. It is, frankly, all so unreal and completely overwhelming. We shouldn't be having to do this. How am I doing this? How are any of us? But the others are doing better than me, though we all try to support each other the best we can.

Chapter 4

The Funeral

A creative, loving eager life of 24 years is a full life, just as much as a life of 84 years. And 24 years of Harry has been the most wonderful gift to the world.
Robert Ashby, on hearing of Harry's death

I wake up on the morning of the funeral feeling oddly calm. It's a warm day for the time of year. Jack and Jessie arrive and we wait. I feel as if I'm slightly out of my body, through the shock, trauma, lack of sleep, or all of these things I expect. I go upstairs to finish my make-up and Lily joins me. The funeral car should be arriving in about 15 minutes, but as I stand in front of the mirror looking out of the window, I see the heart-stopping sight of the funeral director already walking down the road, in his top hat, tails and a cane, leading the hearse. My legs start to give way as I see my son's coffin inside and his photograph behind it. This just can't be right, not my Harry… I'm just not sure I can do this, it's way too much, I'm not ready. I start to crumble. Lily is by my side and is being brave, for my sake. I am proud of her, my living child.

My amazing, wonderful, precious boy is really gone and we somehow have to get through this day. We must, we have to honour him, celebrate the life he had and how very much he was loved. Lily and I join the others downstairs and tell them that Harry is here. I am shaking as I walk through the front door and we all silently get into the car. I look at Harry's photograph in the hearse ahead of us and I'm having trouble comprehending what we're actually doing. We drive slowly to the church; through the streets that Harry walked down so many times throughout his life. We're early. Some of Harry's friends are outside the church having a cigarette. Jack stays with them to help carry in the coffin and Anthony, Lily, Jessie and I are told to go into the church. There are already lots of people and we become the focus of hushed attention as we make our way to the front pew. Photos of my gorgeous boy are being projected onto screens and the songs we have chosen and loved together are being played. I feel pleased – this is what I wanted.

But then panic begins to rise – where is Mum? The friend reading my eulogy is collecting her but neither of them are here. Has something happened? Has the shock been too much for Mum? I turn to a friend and ask if she knows where they are but she shakes her head. I can't concentrate and I'm worried. How can they be late for Harry's funeral? Then I remember the funeral cars came for us early, but this doesn't assuage my fears. No one in the church is speaking and everyone is expecting the service to start because we, the chief mourners, are now here. I must tell someone not to start without them. My anxiety levels are rapidly stepping up – and then they arrive. But this is not a great start, I think.

I hear the start of 'Beautiful Boy' by John Lennon. Oh God, no... this is it then... I really don't think I can do it... I start to break down. People stand and begin to cry as Jack and Harry's friends carry the casket down the aisle, the blue and cream flowers woven through the honey-coloured wicker and the lovely flowers from the bouquet on top cascading over the sides. It looks the way I had hoped it would. I think Harry would approve – nothing formal, a bit unconventional and very beautiful. Just like him. I hear people sobbing uncontrollably behind me.

The vicar says something to welcome us all and we sing 'Morning Has Broken' with a small ensemble of singers who seem to appear from nowhere. No one else really seems to be singing, but I do, loudly, as if doing so might help me feel better. I break down at several points during the service but then seem to be able to pull myself together. I'm in between Anthony and Lily and we hold on to each other. The vicar has told us beforehand that people should speak for no more than a couple of minutes each. Consequently, the service seems to go by very fast and suddenly the next set of friends are going up to carry the coffin out of the church. We follow behind to a Rex Orange County song. I love this song and it reminds me of us being on holiday together in Majorca. Bizarrely, when I hear it start, I have an urge to dance. I realise people might be concerned if I did, so I don't. I try to catch people's eye as we go out, to smile at them, but no one seems to want to look at me. Their upset is palpable, and this is oddly reassuring. Harry mattered; Harry is a loss to this world.

The church hall is packed, and I feel a tidal wave of love towards us, buoying us up and helping us survive this formidable day. I stand in one place and people just come up to me for the next hour or so. Everyone seems to think it was a very lovely and moving service and I am glad to hear this. I've told a couple of friends in advance to make me eat something but I can't really manage it. Eventually, I start to flag and hope that it's nearly time to head off to the crematorium.

I am surprised that there are a couple of friends who haven't spoken to me. This is my first experience of how let down you can feel, how disappointing people are. How they, for whatever reason, cannot handle your visible pain, your terrible loss. You naively assume they might put their own much smaller discomfort aside, at least momentarily, in order to show some compassion for the magnitude of yours, but it seems they don't.

I go up to one of these friends, as she hasn't come up to me, but she clearly feels awkward and doesn't know what to say to me. Another friend of over 25 years, who I actually chose to read a poem at the service, tells me that she, her blank-faced husband and bored-looking adult children won't be coming to the crematorium after all. She tells me flippantly that her daughter has a hangover. Later, I will feel stunned at her need to tell me this at my child's funeral. Our children used to play together and we stayed with them at their holiday home many times. I find myself saying, 'Please come to the crematorium, Harry would want you there,' and then, and I'm really annoyed with myself for this: 'The crematorium is on your way home.' As if coming to my son's cremation is the equivalent to dropping off at the shops when you're rushed and would rather get back. I realise that stupidly I've now given them no choice but to come.

Set against these upsets is the heartfelt compassion emanating from everyone else. Later, I hear from friends that the love for Harry and for us was tangible and that they'd never witnessed such immensity of feeling before. That they were touched by the respect, maturity and humour shown by Harry's friends, despite their obvious pain. That Lily and Anthony were admirably brave to get up and speak. That I looked very tiny and fragile, that they feared my legs would not hold me up.

We get back into the car and head off for the crematorium. When we arrive, we are ushered into a side room where we wait with some family friends. I shake as I stand there and feel somehow removed from what's coming next. Eventually, everyone goes in ahead to the chapel with their individual flowers (to represent what Harry means to them) and six more of Harry's friends pick up his casket as the family wait behind with our roses and Lily's lily. I think I must actually smile for some reason because I catch the vicar's eye and he appears concerned, realising that I haven't quite grasped the momentousness of this stage of the proceedings. Soon, I do.

The pews are literally overflowing with people as we walk into the swell of the heartbreaking soundtrack of *Cinema Paradiso* (a film Harry got us to watch together one holiday when he was a teenager and which we all loved). It's too much and I can hardly breathe as we move into the front pew. I have to hold on to steady myself. People are sobbing behind me. It all seems to have stepped up another gear from the church service; everything feels very highly charged. The vicar starts speaking and looks at me when he says: 'This is going to be brutal.' And it is...

After he says some prayers, one by one, everyone goes up to lay their flower on Harry's coffin. I notice 'blank-faced husband' and 'bored adult children' take their turn, looking like this is all a massive inconvenience to them and I am hurt again on Harry's behalf. But there is a huge mountain of flowers now and it is beautiful and touching, with the music seeming to crescendo.

Finally, only we, the family, are left in the chapel and we go up to add our flowers. I can't seem to fully discern what's happening, yet I find I am wailing and hanging on to the coffin. I know this is goodbye, the last we have of Harry in bodily form. I know his soul isn't in the casket but it still feels that my heart will crack open as I brace myself to leave behind my son's body – the body that I carried for nine months inside my own. The body I helped to grow and nurture to eventual adulthood. His lanky frame, his floppy blond hair, his handsome face, pale skin with still barely any facial hair and that smile... His cheeky grin and laughing eyes, his lovely voice saying, 'Hey Mum', something I will never hear again. His sensitive hands with their artistic fingers and long arms that frequently wrapped me in the best hugs... all now gone... how can it possibly, possibly be true?

Anthony bravely stays to close the curtains in the final act of farewell and then we walk outside. Everyone stops talking as we move through them to see the flowers people have sent. I cannot stand now. Anthony and Lily hold me up. There is complete silence. Eventually, we realise there is nothing left to do and we move to the car. I get in, curl up and whimper all the way home. The others don't speak.

Mum and I go into the house whilst the others go on to the pub for the wake. Two of my close friends come to be with us, make tea and give us leftover cake. One brings me a book about grief which she has already read in order to better understand what I'm going through and the other gives me a necklace in a box within which she has placed cut-out sentences from my eulogy. I continue to be moved by the kindness and thoughtfulness towards me. I expect to feel relief that it's all over – but of course, I don't.

When they've gone, I text a friend who has gone to the wake to see how Anthony and Lily are faring and she gives me updates – Anthony is talking to everyone and Lily, although breaking down at times, is being looked after by Tom. Eventually, they come home with several large collages of images of Harry and his friends that were put up at the pub. Anthony is strangely euphoric with alcohol and the tidal wave of love he has witnessed for his son. I think I might sleep now, but unfortunately I don't. This won't improve for a while; the shock still firmly embedded in my body and mind shows no sign of dissipating yet.

I hear later from one of my oldest friends who lives in Los Angeles. Despite the time difference, she stayed up during the night, keeping vigil alongside her mother-in-law and sister, sending us love and healing energy during the time we are going through Harry's funeral. We appointed this friend to be one of Harry's godmothers when he was born but once she moved to the States, she rarely saw us or him over the intervening years. Despite this, she is affected by his loss and, like many others, feels a strong connection to him.

Chapter 5

The Descent

My world falls apart, crumbles, 'The centre cannot hold.' There is no integrating force, only the naked fear, the urge of self-preservation. I am afraid. I am not solid, but hollow. I feel behind my eyes a numb, paralysed cavern, a pit of hell, a mimicking nothingness.

The Unabridged Journals of Sylvia Plath

Now the funeral is over, I feel the need to withdraw. More of the pain starts to seep through. I am so very, very traumatised. The day after the funeral, in my continuing sleep-deprived, surreal, slightly delirious state, I have a powerful image in my mind of walking slowly down some steps, resigned, like a descent into hell, into Dante's inferno, with no choice in the matter and no way back.

I have a dream in which Anthony and I are walking down a road where eventually there are no more street-lights. It's getting darker and darker but, for some reason, we can't turn back and have to keep moving forward, despite not being able to see where we're going. We are quietly fearful as we walk blindly into the unknown, unable to guess what lies ahead of us. I find it's not very difficult to interpret the meaning of this particular dream.

Eventually, I start to eat again, though I seem to have completely forgotten what meals I used to make and have no inclination to cook anyway. We are still being brought food occasionally, which is a much-appreciated lifeline, but otherwise, for now, we rely on ready meals or Deliveroo. I don't care at all really, but I do momentarily feel better physically when my blood sugar comes back into balance after I've eaten something. My whole career as a nutritional therapist was based on eating well and now it's all been completely abandoned. However, I don't want to get ill, so I manage to take supplements and continue to do what I can to calm my nervous system and persevere with my attempts to improve my sleep.

I feel a lot of confusion as to why Harry is gone and why my life has been so monumentally devastated as a result. Up until now, I have very much believed in the power of positive thought, manifesting and the law of attraction. Well, I didn't 'manifest' this horror story due simply to being 'out of alignment'. It's easier, I bitterly conclude, to apply this belief system to less apocalyptic events in life. My life was not full of negativity leading up to Harry's death, so why am I now in a living hell and my son tragically dead? I just want to make sense of it but now everything I believed in seems thrown into question. Does everything happen for a reason? If so, what can the reason for this possibly be?

Many of the inspirational quotes that come up on my social media feed now really annoy me. In fact, I feel furious, especially when it comes to the promotion of the belief by many motivational speakers and self-help gurus that 100% of our experience in life depends on whether our thoughts are positive or negative – because 'our thoughts create our reality'. How can this *always* be the case? This implies that, in theory, I have created the terrible pain and trauma that I'm currently living with solely from my negative thinking; that I created, and am responsible for, this harrowing experience of being a bereaved mother. But there are things that happen in life that are beyond our control, that we have no power over, not least because other people have free will, so it's impossible to control everything with positive thinking and you most definitely cannot 'manifest' someone else's death by having negative thoughts!

Practising non-attachment to what happens to you in life,

which I also so often see advocated, isn't being spiritually evolved in my view. Spiritual beliefs should surely not be used to avoid dealing with pain such as this. I don't believe that can be healthy. I simply can't rise above this agony right now, or maybe ever, but I don't believe this means I'm less evolved or a failure because these emotions currently overwhelm me. Later I read that there can be a very real danger that the 'cult of positivity' may be used to silence the human experience, minimising what happens to others with feelgood statements and the dismissal of difficult emotions. This is certainly beginning to resonate. We simply can't be positive if something really tragic happens to us and it's most certainly not always a situation that we attract through our negative thinking.

Harry's Room

I have heard it said that the greatest loss a human being can experience is the loss of a child. This is true. It doesn't just change you, it demolishes you. The rest of your life is spent on another level.
Gloria Vanderbilt

Three weeks after Harry dies, we have to clear his flat. I can't help but torture myself with the thought that he probably wouldn't have died if he had still been living at home. I would have checked on him, I would have saved him.

Even though it's the last place he was alive, I don't feel much of a wrench that we will never again visit the place. We throw some things away, including the bedding that he died in, but we pack up most things to bring home to his childhood bedroom. His friends help us bring it all back and his bedroom is now bursting at the seams. This is all we have left of Harry in material form and everything he owned suddenly becomes very important. This is the entirety of his life; there will be nothing more now. He touched these records, wore these clothes, lay on this cushion, used this toothbrush.

I wash his underwear and jeans and put them in the chest of drawers I painted cobalt blue when he was little. If I look very closely at the wall above his fireplace, I can see the faint outline of the rainbow he asked me to paint for him the summer he was 5. I don't wash his dirty sweatshirts and T-shirts because they have his smell and, excruciatingly painful as that is, this scent keeps me connected to my boy in a very primal way.

Over the coming weeks, I spend a lot of my days on his bed, weeping and desolate. I try to remember him at different ages; that's all I have now. There will be nothing after 24. There will be no new memories. I look at his things, smell his clothes and talk to him, beseeching him to explain how his not being here any longer can possibly be true. I read a quote by Donald Hall who says that you think their death is the worst thing that could happen. And then they stay dead. It's hard to explain just how accurate this feels.

We used to call Harry the 'cat whisperer' because he appeared to have a hypnotic effect on both our cats and they loved him best out of all of us. Once he moved out, they completely took over his bedroom, Ziggy inhabiting the wardrobe and Bibi his bed. Now that I spend a lot of time sobbing on Harry's bed, Bibi and I develop a special bond. She's always been very timid and not particularly affectionate but now when I cry, she nuzzles my head and purrs and I find this remarkably soothing. She will also suddenly stop and seem to look at something behind me and stare at it and then follow it as if it's moving. I like to think she's sensing Harry's presence – his ongoing living energy – and this thought sometimes alleviates a little of my torment. Although I don't sense him yet, I just can't believe he's not here with me in some form.

I think about how much harder it would have been if he had died at home in his bedroom. If he had to die, then I am actually grateful that I'd experienced a short period of time without him beforehand, in order, at least, to get used to his absence in the house, to not seeing him on a daily basis. The house was so quiet after he moved out – no yelling at him to turn his music down, and there was less washing to do, less mess in the kitchen. But I did miss him terribly, despite knowing it was a natural progression now he was earning enough money to live independently, and I felt so lucky that he was only moving a couple of miles away and I could still see him regularly. I remember reading an article called 'The Crushing Grief of An Empty Nest' soon after he moved out. How absurd, I now think, that some journalist should equate the normal stage of your child leaving home with an actual soul-wrenching bereavement.

A few weeks after Harry dies, it's my birthday. Usually, we would go out for a family meal but now I barely leave the house. How could we possibly go out, just the three of us? I don't want to mark the occasion, but others do and are sensitive to how hard the day is for me so soon after he has gone.

When I look in the mirror, a hollow, visibly traumatised version of myself looks back. I feel as if I am shattered into a million fragments, sharp and fragile, but my belief in the afterlife is growing out of this devastation. I had always had non-religious spiritual beliefs, but now it all seems so obvious to me that there must be something else and that energy surely must continue on, just in a different form. After all, scientifically speaking, energy can't die. I desperately want some sign from Harry, but someone says to me that my grief is very dense, so my vibration won't be high enough to sense him. I decide to find a medium. This idea lifts me slightly, as does the prospect of bereavement counselling.

I continually wonder how it is that I haven't died of a broken heart. I have a constant ache there and I sigh and catch my breath all the time. I yearn for Harry and so desperately want to be with him, but I know that I can't kill myself because of the pain it would cause others. Nevertheless, I'd definitely prefer not to be here. There is no doubt that part of me died when Harry did. Perhaps that part now resides with him. I'd like that to be true – I don't like to think of him on his own.

I know everyone is worried about me. Anthony and Lily are coping better than I am but Mum has 'survivor's guilt', wrestling with why she is still alive at 87 when her 24-year-old grandson is dead. I know she also struggles to see her daughter suffer so profoundly. Within four days of losing Harry, she loses half a stone and her blood pressure rockets. Now she is starting to feel some pain in her body and over the coming weeks this gets steadily worse.

The Bereavement Counsellor and the Medium

Some souls come into our lives for only a short time.
They come to touch our lives with love and open our hearts.
They go home because they didn't need long to accomplish their mission.
Once those bonds of love are formed, they transcend this life, lasting for eternity.
Nothing is ever lost.
Love never dies.
Claire Broad

In the same week, I see both a bereavement counsellor and a medium. I feel like my grief is overpowering Anthony and Lily's grief, so I decide that seeing a counsellor might give them both a bit of a break from my acute distress, the extremity of which must feel terrifying for them at times. The route to the counsellor takes me past Harry's old school and I keep seeing kids walking past in his school uniform. I envisage him walking along in that uniform as a stroppy teenager, tall and skinny with his bright blond hair marking him out, and I feel such intense love for that boy. I arrive early and sit in the car crying. I feel so angry that life has put me in the position to warrant bereavement counselling. This was not meant to happen to me, this is not the life I was supposed to have.

When I go in, we don't get off to a very good start. I ask if I can use the loo before we begin but apparently, I can't. The therapy room is in the garden and the counsellor doesn't like people to enter the house where the toilet is. I feel annoyed and hope my bladder will hold. I will just have to leave early if it can't. I assume the counsellor will have information about what kind of bereavement I have experienced and that it was only five weeks ago. Clearly, she hasn't as she starts going through a standard questionnaire which includes questions such as, 'On a scale of 1 to 10 how is your social life?' and 'On a scale of 1 to 10 how are you at work?' This just seems so wildly, laughably inappropriate as I sit there, a newly bereaved mother who rarely leaves the house! But I'm here now so I may as well tell my story and see what the session can offer me. I weep profusely throughout, using a lot of her tissues. She looks genuinely moved and says as much at the end of the session. She is kind and I decide to let go of my annoyance about the questionnaire and lack of toilet facilities.

In total I have four sessions, but – in the end – I decide that sitting and stewing in my grief for an hour each week isn't what I need right now. I suppose I'm lucky I already have people who I can talk to in such depth that these sessions don't really offer me much in addition. I'm also used to a more proactive way of working as a coach, so I conclude that I am probably better suited to this sort of support.

Later that week, I see a medium over Skype. I have chosen carefully. This is a woman who has written several books, has a Masters in Philosophy and has taken part in psycho-spiritual research. She starts by telling me I'm very intuitive, with a 'porous energy' (the latter doesn't sound like a good thing). Then we get on to Harry. She is surprised he's coming through so early after passing over. She's very matter of fact and tells me that it was his time to go, that his soul was never planning to be here for long. She confirms what we know, that he died unexpectedly but he didn't take his own life. She says he went because he had done all he needed to do in this lifetime. He was never going to grow old. I find that, surprisingly, this makes perfect sense to me. Much as I would give anything to have seen Harry get married, become a parent (and he would have been a great one) and progress in his career, I could never quite see it, not like I can for Lily.

The medium tells me Harry says: 'Mum, I'm alright' and that he's around me, that he always will be and I will feel his presence when the pain is less raw. She predicts (correctly) that the inquest won't be for several months and we will, in the end, feel it's just a formality. She tells me I will eventually find purpose in life again and use what has happened for good in some way. She reassures me that I will feel joy again. There is so much love coming from Harry and we will always be linked. Every time I think of him, he will draw near. I feel consoled and somewhat strengthened afterwards, in a way I didn't after the bereavement counselling.

In fact, for the rest of the day, I am really quite uplifted. I knew Harry wasn't completely gone and now that's been confirmed! It means so much to hear that he's okay. I speak to a couple of my spiritually open-minded friends and then to Lily who is also interested in the possibility of life after death. As we sit in her room, we see lights flickering on the wall. We look for where they must be coming from but there is no sun, and the ceiling light and side lamp are off. The light keeps stopping and starting. It's Harry, we agree, and the flickering continues to the point where Lily is getting freaked out. We say how very like

Harry to find out he can do something and then keep repeating it until the novelty wears off!

But then I crash, and badly. He's still not here in the way I want him to be and I dive down alarmingly into the pain and despair.

Chapter 6

The Problem with Sudden Death

There are people you love, who can't stay forever,
and there will be things you can't fix, although you are clever.
Matt Haig, *The Truth Pixie*

The grief is now becoming firmly embedded in the marrow of my bones. I hate that I can't make it better. My default mechanism is to fix things. But this can't be fixed and it can't be made better. I'm finding it very hard to stay in a world without Harry and even though I have to go on for Lily, Anthony and my mum, sometimes even that doesn't feel enough to keep me here.

Lily describes everything as tainted and this is heartbreaking to hear. She will often leave the house when she just can't cope with my bouts of crying. But I feel powerless to hide my pain – my grief has a life of its own that I simply can't seem to control. It's all-consuming, it takes me over. But it's very frightening for Lily to witness and I feel guilty about this. When I am able, I tell her how much I love her and try to reassure her that I can still be her mother, be strong for her, listen to her, support her. And I tell her she needs to know there is always room for her grief, that I know this is terrible for her too.

But she wants me to be who I was before Harry died and I know that version of myself has gone forever. I can no longer be a mother to Harry but, cruelly it seems, I can't be much of a mother to Lily any more either – though I very much want to be. She feels anger towards me because she's scared to see me in such an unfamiliar state. All of this causes us both additional pain. But I currently have neither the emotional capacity nor the energy to do much about it. Most of the time I am barely keeping myself afloat. It feels as if the loss of Harry is destroying me and what's left of our family. I struggle to make sense of him not being here and it just feels like some terrible mistake. I'm finding it so very hard to live this new unwanted life. I try to take it day by day, if not hour by hour; otherwise, I could certainly go mad with grief.

Mother's Day

There it goes again. That heavy feeling in your chest when you don't feel any desire to speak or move. All you want to do is close your eyes and sleep because the process of being broken is incredibly exhausting. You attempt your best to make your days fulfilling but no matter how hard you try, you can't seem to connect to anyone or anything.
Unknown

A few days before Mother's Day, I have my first dream about Harry. It's said that coming into your dreams is one way that a loved one can communicate with you and that if it feels vivid and real then it's likely this is the case. This dream is particularly vivid and feels very real. Harry is using his keys to get in through the front door but there are several heavy chairs placed against the door. He manages to get in and I'm surprised to see him, considering he's dead. He is carrying a bouquet of flowers in one arm and a baby in the other. He seems to be in a rush. He puts them both down and gives me a hug, wishes me Happy Mother's Day and says he's just going upstairs to get something from his room. I wake up abruptly and feel both ecstatic and distraught, the yearning for my boy beyond endurance.

Lily understands how difficult Mother's Day is for me now but wants me to know that she should still be able to 'celebrate' it with me even if Harry can't. She gives me a thoughtful present of a keyring with H and L charms on it. I try to focus on the fact that I am still a mother with a living child and also that I am fortunate enough to still have my own mother. So, we decide to go out for a walk and for tea. As we walk through the park, we see the tree Harry used to fearlessly climb to the very top, and I think of all the afternoons we spent here when Harry and Lily were younger. But I'm okay with that because those memories are somehow intact and unchanged by his death and anyway, I have overlaid them with meeting friends here on our own, without our kids, in recent years.

Mum has to sit down; the physical pain she has been suffering since Harry's death is steadily increasing. She has booked to see her GP the following week. Whilst Anthony goes into the café to get the tea and some cakes, Lily, Mum and I sit outside and my mood rapidly plummets. I desperately want to go home but this Mother's Day isn't all about me and I will have to stick it out. We don't really talk and I feel bad for Lily and my mum that I've made it an awful day for them too, but I am helpless to do anything about it. I hate what my life has become.

Sudden Death

And can it be, that in a world so full and busy, the loss of one creature makes a void so wide and deep, that nothing but the width and depth of eternity can fill it up.
Charles Dickens

As time passes and I read more and more books on grief and maternal bereavement, I come across the particular complications of sudden death. The shock, the disbelief, the lack of being prepared for such a cruel and devastating blow, not getting a chance to say goodbye, the unanswered questions. Your life literally changes in an instant. The impact of a sudden death feels absolutely catastrophic, and so much worse if it's the sudden death of your child.

If Harry had to die, then as his mother, I should have been

with him as he left this life, just as I was when he entered it. We have no idea whether we have done what Harry would have wanted at his funeral or if he is okay with how we plan to memorialise him; we have to guess. We never had a conversation with him about death, let alone what he might want afterwards, because why would we? I know he knew how much I loved him, but I would like to have held him and told him, one last time, as he left...

I keep reading that grief is likely to be prolonged and complicated when it's the death of your child and therefore 'out of order' and if, in addition, it's sudden. I have read that, in these cases, the first year is really about dealing with the shock and that only in the second year do you actually start grieving properly. My heart sinks at the thought. I feel trapped, there's just no escape, how can I possibly get through this. I desperately want it all to stop.

The Compassionate Friends

I cannot think of anyone stronger than a mother who has lost a child and still breathes.
Robyna May

A friend has told me about The Compassionate Friends, an organisation for bereaved parents. I find their site and it is a mine of information covering everything you might want to know about this previously unknowable and devastating situation, whatever age your child was and however they died. I decide to ring the helpline and I speak to a lovely woman who lost her son, also 24 years old, ten years ago. I find it really helpful to hear her story and even though she is crying as she talks, she reassures me that although the loss always hurts, the intense pain and shock that I am currently feeling does eventually lessen. I need to hear this as I have read so much from parents saying the grief is just as bad three, five, ten, 15 or 20 years down the line, to which I can only think: *Kill me now*. The woman tells me there are monthly local Compassionate Friends meetings. Anthony and I decide to find one.

The fatigue from grieving, along with actual lack of sleep, means that going out in the evening is a challenge. As we arrive, we are welcomed to 'the group that no one wants to join'. We are given a cup of tea and another bereaved mother comes to sit beside us. We tell her about Harry and she tells us about her daughter. Another woman joins us who lost her 13-year-old son and I become overcome with emotion that I am unable to control. I go to the loo and have a cry, then go back. I say, 'Sorry, I just felt a bit overwhelmed' and they get it, they truly get it, not just through empathy but because they have experienced it too.

The meeting starts and we all introduce ourselves. When we say our son died seven weeks ago, people who are further along in their bereavement visibly wince. How extraordinary that this group of 15 or so are gathered here, each with their own appalling loss that has devastated their lives beyond all belief, just like us. Children and young adults of varying ages who have died from heart conditions, drowning, drugs, cancer, suicide, murder, medical negligence, epileptic seizure, road accidents. Yet how they died is actually irrelevant because we are simply joined together in the terrible, unspeakable, worst loss of all – that of losing your beloved child.

One parent tells the group how she is organising a meal for her daughter's friends for what would have been her daughter's eighteenth birthday. I am moved by her bravery in undertaking such a task and the awful sadness of it. I start to break down. How embarrassing – this is not about me – but a box of tissues is passed and everybody understands.

At the end of the meeting, we're given yellow roses, which everyone receives in their child's birthday month. A simple, thoughtful gesture to acknowledge your child will always have a birthday, whether you can celebrate it with them or not. What I quickly realise in the meetings we go to in the following months is that some people are trying to make a life around their traumatic loss whilst others seem less able to move forward in their grief several years down the line. Who can blame them when it's so very hard? But I need role models, I want hope because I have to believe it won't always be this bad. I want to see that people can survive this. Somehow. Albeit seemingly against all the odds.

Pain Manifesting in the Body

We have learned that trauma is not just an event that took place some time in the past; it is also the imprint left by that experience on the brain, mind and body.
Bessel Van Der Kolk

Through my work over the years, I have observed that if you are unable to express your emotional pain fully, for whatever reason, the body may do so for you. My mum tries to put on a brave face and is beginning to avoid talking about Harry as she thinks it upsets me. It must be awful to see your daughter suffer, in addition to the loss of your adored grandson. Meanwhile, her physical pain has been steadily increasing and blood tests show very high inflammatory markers. Eventually, she is in so much agony that she cannot even get dressed and it is extremely upsetting to witness. Polymyalgia is diagnosed. In the end, she has no option but to start taking steroids and the pain begins to ease.

Harry's Star

And, when he shall die,
Take him and cut him out in little stars,
And he will make the face of heaven so fine

That all the world will be in love with night
And pay no worship to the garish sun.
Shakespeare, *Romeo and Juliet*

I have somehow survived my birthday and Mother's Day, and the next occasion to bear is Harry's birthday. My darling son, who I can no longer celebrate with, would have been 25 years old. But he's still 24 and will never be older than that. I am now forever denied the opportunity to make his favourite chocolate cake, buy presents for him or tell him stories about the first days of his life. My precious boy who changed the landscape of my life so profoundly the day he was born, and changed it all over again the day he died.

We feel a need to mark the day he came into the world, but I don't feel up to being with other people, so we decide to buy a star dedicated to him. I'm reading a book called *The Afterlife of Billy Fingers* by Annie Kagan and I read that we are literally made of stars and how this isn't just a poetic image but grounded in scientific fact. Although I am well aware you can't really buy a star, I don't care. I like the idea of Harry being immortalised as a star and it feels right. It also gives me a purpose on the morning of his birthday. I have to send the map and details of where his star is to everyone who was important to him in life.

Anthony has to go to work in the afternoon but says he expects to be back by the evening and we plan to get a takeaway as I don't feel up to cooking. In the end, and beyond his control, he doesn't finish until 9 p.m. Lily wants to eat something different, so I sit on the sofa watching television, tears streaming as I eat an Indian takeaway on my own. The abject misery I feel is beyond anything I have ever experienced, and I miss my son so very, very badly.

The generosity of those who pledged money for a bench in Harry's name means that there is a certain amount left over. We donate this to a charity and a music bursary is created in Harry's name. We also buy beautiful pale apricot rose plants from The Compassionate Friends and a slate plaque for the garden inscribed with the following: 'Harry, your light shines on and we will carry you in our hearts forever.' This gives me some comfort and once the roses bloom in the garden, I always have some in a small vase next to the plaque along with some candles.

Marfan Syndrome

Unable are the loved to die.
For love is immortality.
Emily Dickinson

One of the cruel 'added extras' you face when someone dies suddenly – as if you need anything to make the whole experience any worse – is the long wait for an inquest date. We already think we have worked out how Harry died, but one day Jessie, Anthony's older daughter, visits and tells us a paramedic friend of hers had mentioned she has seen several very tall, very thin young men die from unexplained causes in the course of her work. I look into this online and Marfan Syndrome comes up. I start researching and I'm astounded. Harry has many of the signs: unusually tall (6ft 4in), very thin and unable to put on weight, disproportionately long arms, legs, fingers and toes, overcrowded teeth (Harry had four removed) and hyper-flexibility. Marfan Syndrome leads to weakness in the heart and lungs through impaired connective tissues and can be a cause of death in young people, especially smokers. Harry was a smoker.

I speak to someone at The Marfan Association and she tells me it sounds highly probable from the characteristics Harry displayed that he could have had Marfan Syndrome. The only way this can be diagnosed after death is to send off the whole heart and the spleen for an advanced examination of DNA. This, we soon discover, has not been done by the pathologist during the postmortem and so any chance for a formal diagnosis is lost. I feel incredibly frustrated and angry but in order not to completely lose my sanity, I have no choice but to try to find a way to come to some kind of acceptance. If I don't, Harry's death will completely and utterly destroy me. I decide to try to implement something I've been reading about – that it's better to focus not on 'the death' but 'the life'. We are fortunate to have shared our lives with Harry, a true free spirit in many ways – he showed a magical combination of stubborn refusal to do anything he didn't want to, married with sensitivity, creativity and a huge capacity for love. After all, what in life is more important than love? Love doesn't end just because someone dies. I try hard to hang on to this. I will have to if I'm to survive.

Although I still get flashbacks to the horror of seeing my dead child, I also try to remember my first instinctive thought at that time, which was that his body was just a shell. I felt from those first moments that his soul had definitely moved out and could therefore live on in a non-physical form. And if, as the medium said, it was simply his time to go, then how he died is actually immaterial.

I find a quote by John Bramlett who says that when he sees his son's face after he has passed away, he realises there are two possibilities: 'either this tragic world was all there was or there was something far greater beyond this life that I did not yet comprehend...In these rare moments of extreme pain we may sense, just for an instant, that something does lie beyond the mists of this confining physical world in which we live.' I find myself very much relating to this observation and am glad to discover I'm not the only parent who has these thoughts. It does feel as if I had an ephemeral glimpse of something beyond my limited comprehension, a hint of something bigger and infinite, a flash of knowing that this life is not all there is.

Chapter 7

The Bottom of the Sea

On grievers:
*I think particularly about how these people looked when I saw them
unexpectedly...during the year or so after the death. What struck
me in each instance was how exposed they seemed, how raw. How
fragile. How unstable. I understand now.*
Joan Didion, *The Year of Magical Thinking*

By the time we reach around three months after Harry's death, I
am barely leaving the house because of the anxiety I feel. It seems
irrational that the trauma and loss of Harry have manifested
in struggling to go to the supermarket or cafes, getting on the
Tube, going to the cinema or theatre – such simple activities.
I dread seeing anyone in my vulnerable state. I worry that
they might not know what has happened and I might have to
explain, leading me to break down. If they do know, I worry
they might not acknowledge it and that the hurt this will cause
me will mean I will be unable to control my emotions. Given my
fragility, the latter seems highly likely.

Looking back, I recall how a couple of days after Harry dies,
Anthony, Lily and I go to the supermarket in a kind of trance. I
brace myself for seeing Harry's favourite foods but when I spot
an unpredicted Easter egg display, I can't control my weeping.
In the months to come, it becomes more stressful to go, rather
than less so. When I do manage it, I often get back to the car with
the shopping and burst into tears. I feel no sense of achievement
when I complete the trip, just a terrible despondency that my
life is now so diminished.

Anthony and Lily continue to live a more normal life than I
do and can go out. One evening they are both out, separately.

Anthony says he will be back by 9 p.m. at the latest and I expect Lily around 10.30 p.m. When it gets to 10 p.m., I feel anxious and decide to text Anthony. He doesn't respond. In my 'before' life, I wouldn't have worried, but this is 'after' and now I know anything can happen.

I decide to text Lily. She doesn't reply either. I am starting to properly panic and around 10.30 p.m. I text Anthony again. He still doesn't respond. I am now hyperventilating and feeling some of the symptoms I felt on the night we found Harry. My heart is racing and I'm starting to shake. I hear the door. Lily comes in to find me having a panic attack. Eventually around 11 p.m. Anthony returns, having forgotten to check his phone...

Lily then experiences a similar panic when we go to our first Compassionate Friends meeting and have put our phones on silent. I don't check mine until we get in the car and by then it's after the time that I anticipated we'd be home. It's agreed – we all need to be mindful of keeping in touch. Everything is different now. We now know how very unpredictable life can be and how the sand can so easily shift beneath your feet and suck you under. We know that bad things do happen. We're no longer operating as a normal family who have only experienced normal things and normal worries.

Ashes

It is boundless and it is bottomless. The grief and the abyss are infinite.
Bob Geldof

Once the grenade of sudden death has exploded and you're left dazed in your crater of grief, everything just seems to slow down and time takes on a new meaning. Grief seems to leave me paralysed in many ways. It's four months since Harry died and his ashes are still with the funeral directors. Abruptly, I stir from my malaise and say to Anthony that we need to have Harry at home. We have failed to think of a good place to scatter his ashes and now it seems suddenly obvious that he should be back with us and in his bedroom. What on earth took us so long? Now we wonder what to put him in. As with the coffins, the urns all have connotations of old people (who've most likely been lucky enough to live a long life, I think resentfully).

We find a company that can cover a wooden box with images of your loved one. This is what we decide to go for. Unfortunately, when the box arrives, they haven't done a very good job and one of the photos is of just two-thirds of Harry's face. The old me would just be annoyed, contact the company, ask them to do it properly and forget about it. This new me is reduced to tears. I miss the old me but I know she's gone forever. The new me has part of her missing. It's as if I have had several layers of skin removed so that I am now left extra vulnerable, extra sensitive.

Eventually, an improved box arrives and is taken to the funeral directors. However, we haven't, for some inexplicable reason, anticipated how we might feel when Harry 'comes home'. Anthony goes to pick up the ashes and as he walks through the door with the box I am taken aback by my unexpected reaction. I take the box from him and it's heavier than I imagined it would be. The weight of it and the fact that it contains the remains of Harry's actual body completely floors me. I can't believe this is all we have physically, literally, of our cherished boy. There is still so much raw disbelief. We take the box up to Harry's room and sit on his bed together holding it tight. Lily comes to join us, and we all sob inconsolably.

Trauma

Bereaved parents are less afraid to die than any other group of people. Many believe they will be reunited with their deceased

child. Others believe that in death, they will be relieved of the pain of missing their child. Others feel that when their child died a part of them died, so their fear of death dissolved.
Nisha Zenoff PhD, *The Unspeakable Loss*

At 18 weeks, I hit rock bottom. I am trying hard to keep my head above water, clinging to the wreckage, but it takes so much effort, so much energy and I am in too much pain. The trauma is just too great. I've really tried to survive this but it seems I'm not strong enough. I let go. I start to float down, away from the surface, away from the light. There is some very small comfort in letting go. I stop struggling. It's a long way down and as I continue to descend it becomes darker, murkier, but I don't care. I get to the bottom. Twin monsters of self-hatred and despair feed on my raw wound and it doesn't matter to me. Let them. I deserve it. I couldn't keep my son alive. I am a terrible mother.

I contemplate the ways I could end my life. I now understand suicide. It's not selfish. I truly believe that my family will be better off without me. They can get through this tragedy, but clearly I can't. I'm becoming a burden to them, my grief overpowering theirs. They are managing to function, to live some kind of life despite their loss, but I simply can't. They are strong. I am weak.

I stay like this for several days, unable to get out of bed, unable to cope with the extremity of my pain. I can see no point in living if this is how it's going to be. The undertow takes me down further and I am powerless. The darkness has won, obliterating my spirit. Eventually, Anthony suggests we go away for a couple of days. I have no interest but reluctantly agree. I sit still and lifeless in the car. It's raining, obviously.

Collateral Beauty

I see it is the whitest, frothiest, blossomest blossom that there ever could be, and I can see it. Things are both more trivial than they ever were, and more important than they ever were, and the difference between the trivial and the important doesn't seem to matter. But the nowness of everything is absolutely wondrous.

Dennis Potter

Although I was quite young at the time, I remember seeing the writer Dennis Potter say this in an interview before he died, and for some reason it stuck with me. Perhaps dying and grieving have some parallels, because the beauty of the natural world seems heightened for me in the midst of my heartbreak. This is collateral beauty. Something so terrible has happened that anything providing a contrast to the abject misery of my loss, such as the waves of love at Harry's funeral or the wonderment of nature, is felt in a deeper way than ever before. It seems beauty and pain are able to co-exist and it's not necessarily a case of one or the other as I might have once assumed.

So, just when I feel it's too unbearable to go on, something pulls me back from the edge. At this point, that something is going away. This literally saves me. Being in nature, whether the countryside or by the sea, brings me back from the brink. It grounds me, feeds my soul and eases my torment, at least to some degree.

I do feel immeasurable sadness when the seasons change, though, like I've left Harry behind in winter. The counsellor said the bereaved don't notice the seasons when they're grieving but I absolutely do, as a double-edged sword – enjoying their beauty but still left totally bereft that my boy won't see this spring, this summer…

We take several short trips away. On one of these, we discover a very beautiful garden, a kind of secret garden adjoining a church. We see a sign which says it's a garden 'for children who have left this world' and its design, including a carpet of tiny white flowers on a slope, is to convey their ascent to heaven.

What are the chances we, as bereaved parents, should stumble across this peaceful little sanctuary? There are butterflies, feathers and robins in abundance, not only in this garden but everywhere we go. Are they signs? We choose to believe they are, and it eases our heartbreak.

The musician Nick Cave, who lost his teenage son, comments that he couldn't relate to the idea of carrying his deceased child in his heart. So instead, he imagined lifting him from his heart and putting him next to him, beside him. He says this had a powerful vibrational effect and gave him access to an impossible realm where he could form 'an increasingly resolute relationship with the spiritual idea of my lost child', leading him to feel more empowered and unafraid as he allowed his son to accompany him out of his 'boundless grief'. I do both – I feel Harry in my heart but also next to me and this connection, outside of the physical world, is growing ever stronger.

It's a relief that, after hitting rock bottom, I can go through a period of relative calm, like an antidote to the extremity of the agony. A counterbalance to the raging storm that has thrown me to the rocks or pulled me under so that I feel I will inevitably drown in my grief. When this period of calm floats around me like a gentle mist, I am able to feel connected to Harry in a more positive way. I feel him with me sitting on the wall smoking a cigarette, next to me in the car or in a deckchair on the beach with his headphones on. And there is love, so much love. I send it to him and he sends it back to me. I imagine him saying 'Mum, I'm actually spending more time with you now than I did when I was alive!'

Identity and Abandonment

When the young bury the old, time heals the pain and sorrow. But when the process is reversed, the sorrow remains forever.
Joseph P. Kennedy

On the whole, the pervading feeling of wading through treacle, as if my life has been forcibly slowed down and I'm helpless to do anything about it, means most of the time I barely do anything at all. Occasionally someone will ask what I do with my days now and, in all honesty, I'm not sure. They just seem to pass. I read a lot, we go for walks, I visit my mum and friends come round, but it's not my old familiar life, the one I used to have. That life is lost now.

My work has always been important to me and I have spent 12 years building up my practice. Now it's gone. I can barely function and help myself so supporting others is not something I feel able to do any time soon. But I am sad and angry that this part of my identity has been taken away from me. I am furious that I am wasting my time grieving when I could be helping people.

And there is intolerable sorrow too when I occasionally check something on my website and I remember how Harry created it for me, knowing exactly what I wanted, completing it a couple of months before he died. Yes, I had to nag him to get on with it and he drove me mad with his procrastination but how grateful I am that he insisted on doing it for me, despite having a full-time job. I'm glad now that we got the chance to do something together so recently. If only I'd realised it would be the last time that we did.

My feeling of abandonment is growing. How could he leave? He must know that this is potentially an impossible journey for me, our mother and son bond so strong, so fundamental to me and my identity as a mother, and now so brutally and cruelly severed. And yet my overriding feeling is that the bond still exists somehow.

Chapter 8

Signs and Psychics

I feel the presence of my son, all around, but he may not be there. I hear him talk to me, parent me, guide me, though he may not be there. He visits Susie in her sleep regularly, speaks to her, comforts her, but he may not be there...Create your spirits. Call to them. Will them alive. Speak to them. It is their impossible and ghostly hands that draw us back to the world from which we were jettisoned; better now and unimaginably changed.
Nick Cave

I have an overpowering and compelling need to connect with Harry. Some of my friends are atheists but others are open to the idea of life after death. Two of Harry's friends go to see a medium and Harry comes through strongly. They find the whole experience incredible and are excited to share it with me. I am now reading books on after-death communication, the afterlife, reincarnation and metaphysics. This belief that we don't die propels me forward and, ironically, helps keep me alive. I read a book by Theresa Cheung and medium Claire Broad and decide to book a consultation with Claire, only to find she has a very long waiting list. I book instead with an alternative medium that she recommends.

The medium tells me my grandmother is here and that she is very concerned about my mum – she says there is sadness and physical pain around her. She describes my grandmother as having a strong will and not being very warm. Even though this is impressively accurate, I only want Harry and start to feel deflated. My other grandparents then show up and unbelievably she gets the names of both my grandfathers correct! But still, all I want is Harry. Then she tells me they're bringing someone else in. She pauses and then asks if I have a child in spirit. I sigh with relief, he's here. She gets that he's male, though his age is slightly wrong. She describes him as having a lovely energy, a bit cheeky and says he's an old soul with lots of light and love around him. She says we have an extremely strong bond, that he is very close to his family, that he was popular, musical, good with technology, tall, good-looking, compassionate, sensitive, talented, creative, intelligent, generous.

She tells me correctly that he was in his bed when he died, that it was around 2 p.m. and he was lost at first because he didn't understand what had happened. But Anthony's mum and my grandparents were there to meet him and he's fine now. He tells her he sees me sitting on his bed crying, that he's always with me. He says to talk to him and he will try to help me. He wants us to go on holiday after the inquest and shows the medium past holidays we had together. He has seen me looking at shoes online (true) and says: 'Buy them, Mum, treat yourself!'

She says he touched the lives of a lot of people, he was popular with girls but didn't have a girlfriend when he died (true), that he had a period of freedom before he passed over (true, having left home so recently) and that he had charisma. Harry tells her that one of the cats has a tummy upset (true!) and that we have moved some pictures about in his room (true). She asks who Tom is. I say Lily's boyfriend and she tells me Harry's around him, and that Harry says Lily deserves love and happiness, that he's with her a lot. He has so much love for all of us.

There are a few things the medium doesn't get quite right, but about 90% of her reading is amazingly accurate – and in a way, it's the things like the cat's stomach upset, the names of both my grandfathers, the description of my grandmother's character and picking up on my mum's physical and emotional pain that are as impressive as the much longed-for information about Harry. It feels hard to doubt the concept of life continuing after physical death when she has got so much right, and I am so pleased my feeling that Harry is around me is endorsed by the accuracy of the reading.

The medium says he's been showing us signs and I think we have had several that I like to believe are from Harry. When the condolence cards were still up, I am talking with Jessie on the sofa, saying I hope we will have the inquest soon so that we can go on holiday as I feel it would help me. Suddenly three cards fall off the bookshelf. I choose to take this as a sign that Harry agrees (and interestingly this was communicated via the medium). Another time, after reading how spirits can move objects, I ask Harry to move the Amazon packaging that's on the top of the sofa. Nothing happens and I forget about it. Later, however, as I'm watching TV, it falls off.

We see plenty of the more well-known signs – robins, feathers and butterflies – which could be explained away, but one day I'm compelled to go into Harry's room because I feel I will notice something significant. I go in but can't see anything so I doubt my intuition. I then go into the bathroom and while I'm looking out of the window, I see a large butterfly on the windowsill of his room flapping its wings.

And other people believe they have seen signs from him. Mum says she sometimes sees feathers drifting slowly and horizontally outside her window. His ex-girlfriend sees a single red rose randomly bloom in her garden, and on a trip across California, Harry's godmother tells me she's thinking of Harry when she sees hundreds of feathers blowing around on the freeway, but no birds are anywhere to be seen. One day while Lily is visiting my mum, she turns on her grandma's laptop and goes to her emails for her. Strangely, the last email from Harry, which was wishing my mum a Happy Birthday, comes up immediately. Mum hasn't looked at the email since she received it, ten months before. There is just no logical explanation…

There are many reports I've read about interference with

electricity, phones or other devices. Aside from the unexplained flickering lights in Lily's bedroom early on which we both witnessed, Lily also believes Harry removed a song from her playlist soon after he died. She didn't delete it but thought that Harry could have done because he might have seen that the song was making her upset. Music was very much something that connected them.

Lily also experiences one of Harry's songs suddenly playing itself. She rings my mobile to tell me and, as we're talking, I inexplicably hear an automated voice saying, 'The number you are calling has not been recognised.' It keeps repeating randomly during our conversation. Is this just coincidence or is it Harry's way of letting us know he's still around us?

I often feel a sensation around my head and face which is hard to describe. It's as if someone is gently touching me. Sometimes I shiver on just one side of my body as if something is next to me. I'm sure some would put these things down to wishful thinking, but I like to think of them as Harry. And if it comforts me, does it matter? Interestingly, however, I later find on a Facebook group that other bereaved mothers describe these exact sensations. It seems what I experience is not uncommon and I am heartened by this discovery.

My best, most inexplicable sign comes when I am checking emails on my phone one day. My phone begins to scroll backwards through the emails very rapidly and I find I can in no way prevent this from happening. I cannot understand why my phone is malfunctioning in this seemingly erratic way. Eventually, it stops at a group of emails – from eight years ago! I look at the emails and incredibly they all involve Harry. It was the time when he was taking GCSEs and a couple are from his English teacher and Head of Year. Then my heart stops when I see an email from him with the subject title: Lost xxx. I click on it and it has a link to a YouTube clip explaining what the TV series *Lost* was actually about. Harry and I loved *Lost* – it was something we could share during his teenage years – but I found the story confusing, hence the explanation video. I click on it and watch it. When I get to the bit about Jack, the main character, arriving in the afterlife where his father is waiting for him, I get goosebumps. I choose to believe this is Harry telling me he will be waiting for me.

I may be deluding myself, reading into this what I want to believe, but then again, the inexplicable scrolling back of my emails to a cluster of emails about or from Harry is pretty strange...

Continuing Bonds

The continuing bonds model demonstrates that the key to getting past grief is recognising that your relationship with the deceased isn't over, it has just changed. What was once physical is now spiritual.

Theresa Cheung and Claire Broad, *Answers from Heaven*

Ultimately, whether or not I am getting communications from my dead son, I'm still without him in the physical world and that is a form of hell that no belief in an afterlife can take away completely. I need links with him in this world.

Whilst still spending a lot of time with Bibi the cat in Harry's room, I begin to remember there will have been some childhood things I will have kept but put away. One is Bobby the Bunny and another is my most prized possession, a Pokémon card, handmade by Harry when he was 7. I suddenly have a strong compulsion to find these and any birthday and Mother's Day cards I might have kept over the years.

I will have put them somewhere safe. But where? I find the cards easily. The most recent Mother's Day card reads: 'Thanks for being the best, most loving Mum anyone could ask for!!' It breaks my heart, obviously. But I can't find Bobby or the

Pokémon card. Anthony is out and I have a feeling Bobby is in the loft so will probably be found but I turn our bedroom upside down looking for the Pokémon card. I fall to the floor in panicky hysteria. How can it be lost?! I have looked everywhere where I thought it might be. Anthony comes home. He says he will find it. I don't believe him. But then he does. Immediately, and somewhere I have already looked. I don't understand how I could have missed it but I am so happy it's found, though my heart cleaves open even more. On it, Harry has drawn a smiling picture of himself wearing a T-shirt with an H on it.

Name: Harry
Eyes: Blue
Age: 7
Level of love: 100
Attacks: Love Burst, Kisses, Endless Love
Most love on: His Mum
Mums cost: Priceless

My heart is overflowing with love for my beautiful boy. Anthony points out that what he writes is actually rather extraordinary for a 7-year-old – concepts of endless love and the priceless cost of his Mum. Later, I frame the card and have it sitting on my desk, his love consoling me despite its physical absence.

I have taken to wearing one of his coats. It's too big but I turn up the sleeves and I like it. It smells of him. I also wear some of his pyjama bottoms and a sweatshirt. These get washed so lose his precious smell but his room still smells of him, and this both upsets and comforts me in equal measure. I have now put some of his unwashed T-shirts and sweatshirts in a plastic box in order to try to preserve his smell as I've heard it is likely to fade with time and the thought of this is unbearable.

We are unable to let any of his things go. Early on I find some old clean clothes in a bag under his bed which he probably hadn't worn for several years. Knowing there were so many other clothes more recently worn, I let Anthony take them to the charity shop – and immediately regret it and want them back. Every single thing he ever owned is now so precious. I do eventually start to give things to his friends because that somehow feels different. We give away some of his records, which we know he would want his friends to have. I give a shirt to his ex-girlfriend that he bought on a trip with her to Budapest and we give some other clothes to Lily, Jack and Jessie.

I read that one of the essential ingredients for surviving this worst of all losses is to talk about your dead child unashamedly. I also talk directly to Harry, both inside my head and out loud. This helps me feel connected to him – and I'm not the only one, it seems. I discover that my mum, who has one of Harry's beanie hats hanging up by her front door, also talks to him. She says goodbye to him/the hat when she goes out and hello when she comes back. I find it very touching to hear that she does this. Sometimes, I ask Harry specific questions and sometimes I get a reply in my head. Anthony has done this too.

One day when we're having some garden furniture delivered, neither of us can remember where we've put the key to the back gate as we rarely use it. For some reason, I ask Harry and I feel he's telling me to go to the drawer of the butcher's block in the kitchen, even though it seemed unlikely we would have put it there. I rummage impatiently through the drawer and can't find it. Meanwhile, as I search in other places without success, Anthony says he's found it. I don't mention my 'conversation' with Harry but once the delivery is completed, Anthony tells me that he also asked Harry where the key was and felt he told him it was in the drawer of the butcher's block – which is where he found it!

Occasionally, Anthony and I talk about what we would give to have Harry back and the answer is anything and everything

– we would both swap our lives for his in a heartbeat. I find it particularly touching when Anthony says he would trade places specifically for my sake, in order for Harry and me to be reunited, not thinking about the reality of what his own loss would do to me, Lily and the newly traded Harry... but he says it because he hates to see me so broken and understands, obviously first-hand, that in the end there is no loss worse for a parent than the loss of a child. But anyway, it's a pointless activity as there can, of course, be no trade. This is irreversible and that is still very, very hard to accept.

Harry's death has inevitably affected our family dynamic. We no longer feel complete, because a quarter of us is missing. It's as if we only have three legs on our family table instead of four and this makes it feel wobbly and precarious, with the distinct possibility of collapse. We can space the three legs out a little in an attempt to achieve a better balance but still, it doesn't feel as safe and stable as it once did. Since having children, my family have always been the most important aspect of my life, above everything, and so I don't like that we've become a smaller family, an incomplete family, a family with a crucial member missing. And whilst it's hard for Anthony and me as parents, it's also very difficult for Lily to be without someone she has known her entire life, someone who was always so protective of her, right from her birth, who always had her back and was so much kinder than the average big brother.

Searching for Things to Help Me Feel Better and Facing Real Life

On a daily basis, the new me has just one simple purpose and that is trying to survive the loss of my loved one for the loved ones who still need me around.
From Grief to Growth

The mediums help but I need other ways to help me through this. I find a Reiki practitioner. I discover that Reiki calms my nervous system quite effectively and although I cry through the treatments, I do feel better for them, at least for a few days. The practitioner is very good at what she does, works hard to help me and is generous with her time, but I find myself quite upset when she seems to compare the loss of my child to that of her pets and elderly father. She even tells me that we have all lost children in past lives, again seemingly diminishing my loss. But I go back for several months because the Reiki itself helps.

A friend sends me a link to Grief Yoga online. This proves to be an unexpected Godsend and often saves me from going downhill. It is very gentle and the breathing helps allay my anxiety. Sometimes I cry through it, especially on the day I notice the spilt milk marks on the blanket box that are in my eye-line as I sit cross-legged on the floor. They're from Harry's toddler cup and I could never get them off. Now I'm glad I couldn't.

I continue to read books on grief and spirituality, and I find I can also be distracted now by novels and television programmes. I'm sometimes taken aback when I watch something where losing a child is part of a storyline. This is not uncommon because I suppose this is inevitably a subject that naturally provides a rich seam of drama. Often the writing and the acting is good, reflecting fairly accurately what it's like – though not always – but I find I'm surprised when a character says something like: 'Everyone knows that losing your child is the worst thing that can happen to you' and I feel very pleased that this fact is being validated. I read a novel, which is not primarily about child loss, where a character who has lost her daughter says: 'No woman can survive the loss of her child.' She later kills herself and another character repeats the statement, as if confirming this to be true. This doesn't upset me; I'm just glad the repercussions of such an unimaginable trauma are being acknowledged.

Thankfully, a great deal of what I watch and read isn't about the death of a child and so provides some much-needed escapism. I need a respite from the unremitting pain, and I can now sometimes find it. I can laugh, which I have read the bereaved often feel guilty about, but I don't. I know Harry would love to see me laughing and we often talk about how Harry would find something funny. On the whole, though, it's a relentless, gut-wrenching, half-life existence that I lead. But I am trying to keep going, picking myself up off the floor, day after day after day.

Vulnerability

She had given off the impression of hidden damage, of a pot that you could still use but must handle carefully or it might break apart in your hands.
Tracy Chevalier, *A Single Thread*

Although I'm limited in my interactions with the outside world, they can, when I have them, possess the ability to completely floor me and then my vulnerability frightens me. This has been the case from the moment we find Harry dead and there are many incidents that follow that show this sense of exposed vulnerability shows no sign of diminishing. One of the first examples happens a few days after the funeral when I have an appointment for a mole biopsy. Anthony goes with me and I silently weep as the doctor performs the procedure. She is kind and the nurse holds my hand. I am told the results will be back in a few weeks and when that date passes and I haven't heard anything, I ring the dermatology department. The receptionist is clearly having a bad day and tells me how short-staffed they are and how she currently has to come in to work at weekends. I don't really need to know this. She says she will speak to the consultant and ring me back. She does but I miss her call and she leaves me a message saying the doctor would like to see me face to face to give me my results and that I've been booked in for an appointment in three months' time.

Why does the doctor want to see me face to face? This presumably indicates something's wrong because, if not, why can I not have my results over the phone or in a letter? I surely can't be expected to wait three months for them! I ring the receptionist. I can tell by her tone that her day has got worse and she thought she had ticked me off her list. She talks over me saying she left me a message, she can't tell me any more and I just have to wait for my appointment. I say I need to tell her something to pass on to the consultant – I have just lost my son and so it's a lot to expect me to wait three months to find out if I have cancer or not, in view of what I'm currently going through. She appears to ignore what I have told her. I am incredulous. I calmly ask if she heard what I just said. She gets very defensive and starts to shout over me. She refuses to pass on my message. I am finding the rapid escalation rather extraordinary. Lily is with me and starts to cry, terrified she might lose me in addition to Harry, as well as at my increasing distress. Anthony comes in and takes over the phone, trying to placate the receptionist. In the end, he speaks to the consultant. It's not cancer.

Another incident of insensitivity that upsets me is talking to the website provider who insists an authentication code will have to be sent to Harry's phone as that's the number they have associated with the account. I explain that he's dead and we can't get into his phone. He's still insistent. And totally devoid of any compassion whatsoever.

There are many seemingly small incidents that tip me over. On one occasion I'm driving to pick up a friend when I see, as I pass the park, that Harry's memorial bench is starting to be installed. I am somehow not prepared and find I feel a bit emotional. There's nowhere to park when I get to her house, so I stop in the middle of the road momentarily. A driver pulls up towards me in the narrow road and stares at me intimidatingly, expecting me to reverse some considerable distance in order to let him pass. The tears come upon me at his meanness. The friend goes up to his car and talks to him. He reluctantly reverses.

These incidents seem to expose my vulnerability and fragility. As for the so-called friends who have disappeared from my life, which I have read over and over is so common, I cannot explain the hurt I feel. Then there are the people you know less well but who airbrush your dead child out of the picture, not mentioning him, as if, who knows, he's still alive or perhaps never even existed. Those that see you in the street but pretend they haven't and, at the opposite end of the scale, those you don't know but vaguely recognise, who look at you with undisguised pity, a slight head tilt and a half-smile.

I begin to realise that the lack of compassion demonstrated by some on the night we found Harry has impacted my trauma. I read that the circumstances surrounding deaths that are traumatic in nature can be severely worsened by an insensitive attitude from those present. I also learn that yelling at someone who is already in shock and feeling out of control leads to further dysregulation. I try to focus on all the love and compassion we receive, but the cruelty of having to tolerate these affronts, in addition to the shattering loss itself, feels too much to bear sometimes and chips away at my fragility.

The change in my self-esteem is shocking to me. I seem to have no resilience; my self-confidence has never been so low. In some ways, this surprises me, but I suppose if the foundations of your world have been shaken to the core, why wouldn't you be full of self-doubt and fear that you have no idea what you're doing any more? The much-used phrase 'Everything will work out alright in the end' has been proved to be a total lie. How can I do normal things now or ever lead a normal life when one of my children has died? This unexpected traumatic loss has robbed me of any stability I thought I had. It's difficult to trust life now. I feel exposed, skinless; anyone and anything has the power to hurt me, it seems – and that feels scary.

Chapter 9

The Inquest

The candle that burns twice as bright
burns half as long.
Lao Tzu

Harry's friends arrange a music night at an arts club in his memory. I am particularly low when the day arrives but I want to go. Anthony and I want to show our support, gratitude and love. When we arrive, we have our wrists stamped and I laugh and momentarily wish I was young again. But I'm not and the music is, of course, loud and, for me, with my now obvious PTSD (post-traumatic stress disorder), very overpowering. Nevertheless, I am pleased to be getting this glimpse into Harry's world. I stand and chat, trying to hear over the music, trying to keep a hold on my capricious emotions. Some of his friends are doing DJ sets and then there are the live bands, musicians who knew Harry and are playing for free in his honour.

When I hear the first band playing a tribute to him and then everyone cheering, I feel the tears leaking out. I am sitting with one of my friends and her son who gives me a hug, and although he doesn't feel like the lightness of Harry, he has the same height and I want momentarily to pretend it is Harry. He has been Harry's friend since before they could even walk and I break, sobbing on his shoulder.

Anthony and I leave soon after and I sit silently crying all the way home, the pain of missing Harry feeling beyond endurance.

Snakes and Ladders

There is a special place reserved for mothers who have lost their

sons. Theirs is a singular and complex order of torture, unlike any other grief, and the fundamental need to lock oneself away from the world is natural, perhaps necessary. It is a form of self-imposed entombment, adjacent to eternity, where they can better be with the one they lost.
Nick Cave

They say grief is like a game of Snakes and Ladders – you start to climb a ladder, thinking your journey is finally upward bound, when suddenly you find yourself sliding downwards again, back to square one. Grief is certainly not the linear process we are sometimes led to believe it is. There are days when I claw my way up from rock bottom but then, without warning, I find I can't help but sink down again. There are no neat 'five stages of grief', a concept popularised by Elisabeth Kübler-Ross (denial, anger, bargaining, depression, acceptance). It's back and forth, up and down, with frankly no progress made at this point. I have cried every day for six months. I read somewhere that 'grief is like a bull and I'm wearing red'. This is exactly how it feels.

Sometimes I feel Harry with me, and sometimes he feels beyond reach. I experience such conflict between my spiritual beliefs and the more positive mindset I'm trying to (re)cultivate, and the black density of my all-encompassing grief. Even though I believe Harry lives on in a different way, I can still get bogged down by Western society's more prevalent beliefs about death. That this life is all there is, he's completely gone, there was no reason for his death, it was just bad luck, there is no purpose in it, nothing to be learned that will lead to some personal or spiritual growth. I begin to realise that even if people believe in life after death, they probably don't feel they can speak openly about it.

I go from accepting this life isn't all there is and seeing a bigger picture, to being dragged down into very human negative emotions, especially by those (a few I meet but mainly those I read about) who are stuck in their grief years down the line. Those who say it doesn't ever get better, they are still in great pain, their lives no longer have any meaning. I'm aware that beliefs and habits form neural pathways in the brain. The more you reinforce these beliefs and habits, the deeper the groove, the more entrenched they are and the more they become your reality. So, I decide, whenever I am able, that it's better to focus on what brings me the most peace and hope. Sometimes this is easier said than done, however...

One good thing is I now have absolutely no fear of death, which is really quite liberating. Either I'll be with Harry again, which will be amazing, or it will all just be over and I'll be out of this emotional pain – so win-win really. A lot of the time I long for death. When I'm going to sleep, I whisper, 'Please don't let me wake up tomorrow.' Sometimes, though, I want to live until Lily is settled and has her own family. And sometimes I want to live to use this experience for some kind of good so that the pain hasn't been all for nothing. I want to find some meaning in my life again, to help other bereaved parents, with the skills I had and perhaps the new skills I'm acquiring. I feel now I won't live to old age though and secretly that's a relief.

I read that in cases of sudden death, the loss is inevitably disruptive and complicated. In her book *How to Go on Living When Someone You Love Dies*, Therese Rando says that this is because 'the adaptive capacities are so severely assaulted and the ability to cope is so critically injured that functioning is seriously impaired. Grievers are overwhelmed.' It does very much feel as if my mind, body and soul have been in a terrible fight and are all horribly mutilated, that it might be touch and go as to whether they will make it. But they do somehow survive yet another day, despite the alarming wounds.

Unexpected, unexplained sudden deaths inevitably have inquests, the experience of which, together with the wait of several months, only compounds grief and trauma for the bereaved. We request the postmortem and toxicology reports ahead of the inquest. There are drugs in Harry's system, though a relatively modest amount. We know that he would have taken them in an attempt to relieve pain and to get some sleep, unlikely to consider their accumulative effect on a body that was weakened considerably from sleep deprivation and his other underlying issues. In addition, we know that, crucially, there is a very strong likelihood of a weakening of the heart and lungs with Marfan Syndrome.

There is a stark, inhumane barbarity to reading the postmortem report – something no parent should have to withstand. The pathologist gets his height wrong. I am furious at his carelessness. I feel nauseous reading the details and part of me shuts down, the horror that they have cut up my precious son's body just far too much to bear.

The inquest looms over us like a menacing black storm cloud that you know is coming but you don't know when. We have a holiday planned that we booked before Harry died and we ask if there's any chance we can have the inquest before it. I cannot bear the thought of going away knowing we will have to come back to it or the injustice of having to cancel the much-needed trip. To be fair, the coroner's officer says he will bear it in mind, and he does. The inquest is to be held a few days before we are due to go away.

I feel surprisingly calm when the day comes. We have requested a volunteer to be with us and she's very kind. In the end, the whole thing is low-key. We have provided a very in-depth account of our view on what happened and why, including information, evidence and research studies I have found about the effects of sleep deprivation, witness accounts that Harry reported feeling ill, information about his migraines and allergies, plus all that we have gathered regarding Marfan Syndrome. We state that we believe a number of factors came

Love Untethered

together to cause our son's death.

The coroner is compassionate, but when we question why the pathologist didn't send the heart and spleen away to carry out further testing for Marfan Syndrome when Harry clearly had many of its unusual characteristics, he shuts us down by impressing upon us the pathologist's considerable experience. I quickly realise we're not going to get anywhere with this. Marfan Syndrome was not investigated and that can't be rectified now without his body. Usually, I would argue my case, but that was the old me, not the new, bereaved me. What's the point? It doesn't matter. Harry is still dead.

There are no surprises and the coroner rules out suicide. It's all rather an anti-climax. I may feel resigned but Anthony is upset. He has a need to tell the coroner that Harry was very special. The coroner says, 'I can see that.' I understand how Anthony wants this fact to be acknowledged.

We leave the courtroom. It's a lovely day and I try to feel some relief that it's over, that we can draw a line, but I can't seem to manage it.

78

Chapter 10

The First Holiday

And I'd choose you;
in a hundred lifetimes,
in a hundred worlds,
in any version of reality,
I'd find you
and I'd choose you.
Kiersten White, *The Chaos of Stars*

Holidays were important to our family and Harry especially loved them. How lucky were we that, as an adult, he still wanted to come with us. I'm so grateful that we have memories of these happy times together. This particular holiday was only ever going to be just me and Anthony, though, which helps slightly. However, we are going to Normandy, an area we went to many times as a family and I'm worried about leaving Lily at home. We ask her if she'd like to come with us, but she has to work and would rather stay behind with Tom. I also wonder whether it's too long for us to be away. I can't anticipate how being away for more than a few days will feel, with my emotional state being so precarious. But I try to look forward to it. I know Harry would want me to.

As we find a seat on the ferry, a family with a little blond boy come and sit near us. Suddenly, I'm transported back to the ferry crossings we made with our own little blond boy. I try to hold on, to resist being swept away by my sadness. Then I see a teenage boy talking with his mum, in a way particular only to teenage boys, slightly stroppy but only because that becomes their default for a few years. The mum placates him, half exasperated, half good-natured. The familiarity of this relationship unravels me. It's only nine o'clock and I'm already desperately aching for my lost boy...

The sun is shining and the air is warm as we disembark. The familiar countryside, with its half-timbered and thatched houses and its rather flat landscape, that we have driven through so many times before with Harry and Lily in the back of the car, causes me bittersweet pain. As we pull up to the cottage, I am in tears and my heart physically aches. I don't think I can do this. But I do want to. After unpacking, we head off to the supermarket. I have anticipated this will be difficult. Harry loved a French supermarket, filling the trolley with treats of sweets and smiley-faced chocolate biscuits as a child and latterly with beer and crisps.

We park the car and then I remember. Harry always got the trolley. Ever since he was small, we gave him a euro and he would get the trolley. He will never do that again. I hadn't anticipated the searing agony of this small thing and the tears begin once more. Anthony says he'll go in and I can stay in the car. No. I'll keep my sunglasses on; I don't know anyone here and I can cry behind them if necessary. We go in.

I avoid some of the aisles that Harry would make a beeline for and focus on the shopping list I've written. I find that the search for items in an unfamiliar French supermarket distracts me. In addition, I seem to feel less exposed in this environment where no one will know that I'm a mother whose son has recently died. We buy nice food and lots of wine that I feel I may have the potential to actually enjoy. A little progress perhaps.

It's a gorgeous evening and we sit to eat at the long table in the peace of the cottage garden. I think it will help being here. It feels healing. I'm looking forward to the market tomorrow and going to the beach. For a moment, it's as if I'm still living my old life, feeling excited on the first day of a holiday, blissfully unwinding, enjoying myself. But this isn't my old life, this is my new, unasked-for life, full of yearning for what's gone, the pain of my boy being ripped from me, without warning and forever.

The next day, after visiting the market, we go for lunch. There is a moment of anxiety. It's an enclosed space as we're seated inside, but the fact that we won't see anyone we know seems to help and, although I still feel fragile and melancholy, I'm okay. We talk about what we plan to do in the coming days, and I'm distracted and looking forward to my food. But then I think of Harry and just desperately wish he was here with us. As I have this thought, a single pink petal catches my eye as it floats down from the ceiling and lands next to my hand resting on the table. I look up to see where it's come from. There are no flowers or plants in the restaurant. There is nothing to explain where it's come from. It's a sign from Harry, I say. He's with us. And whether this is the case or not, the thought of him being with us on holiday, in any form, seems to give me permission to take some joy where I can.

And for about three or four days, I do actually enjoy myself. The sun, the seaside, the food and being in the countryside, all give me pleasure. We have a church opposite the cottage, and we go in daily to light a candle for Harry. This helps us both to feel connected to him. Anthony particularly takes comfort in this and the tears come more for him than me. We walk around the churchyard and look at the gravestones, seeking out the young ones. Whether they died recently or a century ago, we are not the only parents to lose a precious child.

There is an Englishman next door and one day, as we return from the beach, we chat to him as he trims a hedge. We talk for quite some time about the area and the people who own our cottage. It's small talk essentially and I think: *He doesn't know, he hasn't realised, it doesn't show.* I've marvelled at Anthony's ability to act with people as if nothing catastrophic has happened to him, but this is my first time at holding a conversation at length with a stranger, pretending I'm an ordinary woman who isn't completely traumatised by the death of her son – and I seem to be pulling it off. He has no idea. I'm successfully hiding it and I don't seem to have 'fragile bereaved mother' tattooed on my forehead. This feels like a bit of a milestone because I see how it can be done. I don't necessarily want to have the ability to hold an everyday conversation just yet, but I can see it would be a useful skill if I'm ever to operate again socially.

Eventually, I grow suspicious of this eerie respite from the full-on grief that is now so familiar to me. How long can it last? I feel it lurking dangerously in the background so I try to make the most of any enjoyment I can get. I continue to feel as if Harry is with us, and maybe that's the trick. I take a large white feather that falls from the sky onto my sun lounger, seemingly from nowhere, as another sign that he's here.

And it doesn't last. Towards the end of the holiday the grief, like rumbling thunder in the distance, gets steadily closer until it's overhead and all-encompassing again. But I am grateful for the short respite and hang on to the fact that if it can happen once, perhaps it can happen again.

Dreams

What we once enjoyed and deeply loved we can never lose, for all that we love deeply becomes a part of us.
Helen Keller

Since Harry died, I don't remember my dreams as well as I used to, but I still get a sense that my subconscious is working through the effects of the trauma as I sleep. At least I hope so. I know from my work, and from my reading on grief, that both physical and emotional healing can take place as we sleep. Thankfully, I generally sleep so much better now than during the very early months and that means my energy is better and I feel physically stronger. I have never once had that feeling people refer to of forgetting, for a moment when you first wake, the terrible thing that has happened. I never forget – not even for a second.

They say dreams are one of the easiest ways for loved ones to communicate with us as we are more receptive when we're asleep. Frustratingly, I have very few dreams about Harry, or at least not ones that I remember. The ones I do have though are vivid, like the one I had just before Mother's Day. Now I have another vivid dream, of walking barefoot up an escalator that's very steep and not working. The escalator is there instead of the steps in the auditorium of a theatre. More than halfway up the rows of seats, I see Harry's tall frame and blond hair and he's wearing a familiar grey hoodie. He's in the aisle seat (as always, to accommodate his long legs) and he gets up to let me in to the seat next to him. We hug and I seem to be able to lean on his shoulder (so he's not as tall as he really was). I say 'Why did you go?' and 'If your life is over, my life is over.' It feels imperative to make him understand so that he doesn't die again.

I suppose the steep escalator that doesn't work represents my uphill struggle, my bare feet my extra sensitivity, but I don't know why Harry is less tall. The conversation where I try to impress upon him not to die again is perhaps a throwback to attempting, usually in vain, to get him to do his homework, revise for exams, eat vegetables, tidy his room, but also just because seeing him alive makes me so desperately want to persuade him not to go now that I have him back.

In another dream, I don't see Harry but I know it's him. I feel an enveloping hug from behind me, an enormous palpable energy and a sense of being lifted. I feel euphoria and so much love. I read that this is not an uncommon experience and that it can feel incredibly real.

I find it interesting that I don't seem to have nightmares, though perhaps that's because my waking life feels like one, but I do have a rather interesting anxiety dream. I have it twice, so

I guess my subconscious is trying to tell me something. I come abruptly to the edge of a sheer cliff. It's very high and I look down and see the sea far beneath me. I am teetering on the edge and desperately trying to keep my balance. There is a feeling of having no way back when suddenly I see before me a piece of land that, if I am brave enough, I might be able to jump over to. It's a risk, I might fall and I'm terrified, but I know I can't go back. Then I wake up. I suppose this is about my fear of the future, about losing my grip and perhaps having no choice but to leap forward into the next stage of my life. The part without Harry.

As the summer rolls on I definitely find being outside in the sunshine can ease my sorrow temporarily. I go for walks with people or sit reading in the garden by Harry's plaque. It's still a struggle to get through the days, to keep constantly pulling myself up from the pit of my desolation. Sometimes, I can carry the pain for a while only for it to crush me under its weight yet again.

One of Harry's friends puts some of Harry's music on Spotify. I'm very pleased but I just can't listen to it. It's too painful at this point, but I have hope I will be able to eventually. I haven't been able to listen to any music since Harry died, let alone his own. But I'm very appreciative that it's there. It's his legacy and I'm so glad we have it.

On the six-month anniversary, Jessie does a gym challenge to raise funds for Harry's charity. She does five classes at different gyms across London and runs between them. It's quite a feat and I'm grateful to Jessie and her two friends who carry out the challenge with her. Because I don't feel able to tackle the Tube yet and haven't been into central London for six months because of PTSD, we drive to Victoria to watch the final class, in which Lily and Tom are also going to participate. Harry's music is going to be used for the class.

Anthony has got the time wrong and we arrive early. The

girls are still running from the last gym, and I feel vulnerable and overwhelmed in this noisy environment. Finally, they arrive and I give them each some flowers before going in to watch the class. I imagine Harry sitting next to me as we listen to his songs being blasted out. It feels like a lot for me, but I am so proud of Jessie and full of admiration for undertaking this for her little brother.

When we come out Anthony and Jack are talking and laughing with some people Jessie knows – a friend of her mother's and some old school friends. I immediately feel on edge at the inappropriateness of this. What are they doing here? I find it very hard that these people didn't even know Harry and seem to be completely insensitive to the whole purpose of why we are here. No one says to me: 'I was very sorry to hear about Harry,' no one even mentions him and, as they all cheerfully sit down together, as if it's an everyday social gathering, I feel the tears coming and the panic rising. The lack of control I have over my emotions frightens me. This is why I struggle to leave the house unless it's somewhere outside and I'm able to move away easily, to escape people who might hurt me, opening my raw wound further.

There is talk of us all going for a pizza. I can't do small talk with these people who are ignoring Harry's existence; this won't be possible for me. Nor, actually, do I think it should be, considering the circumstances of why we're here. I get up and walk away before the tears engulf me. Anthony and Jack follow. I say that I can't be with people I don't know, least of all ones who aren't even acknowledging Harry and the actual purpose of the gym challenge.

These people must see I'm upset because they leave, and we go for a pizza with Jack, Jessie and Tom. We sit outside so my anxiety is at bay again, but it's hard to have this family gathering without Harry. It all just hurts so much.

A few months later I talk with Jessie about how I felt and

she understands this, saying she felt awkward that these people turned up and that they didn't acknowledge the circumstances of the occasion. I discover from talking to other bereaved parents that extraordinary insensitivity and lack of compassion towards the grieving seems to be a common issue, adding such unnecessary insult to injury.

The Unravelling Continues

There will always be a hole in your heart the shape and size of your child.
Angela Miller

I read somewhere that, in order to give yourself a break, you can imagine putting your grief in a box up on a high shelf. You know it's still there and you will inevitably take it down again – in fact, it would be unhealthy not to – but it just gives you a little respite from the pain. I try to keep focused on enjoying small things in order to get through the days: nice food, the sunshine warming my face, a good Netflix series. But it's sad this is what my life has come to. My world has shrunk. I sometimes think I'm getting closer to being able to start work again but then a tidal wave of grief knocks me to the ground and I wonder at my naivety.

My heart continues to literally hurt, my chest feels tight, I catch my breath. At seven months, I am desperately sick of grief. I feel trapped by it, drained and exhausted. My grief is still so raw and visceral. Why, when my heart is so terribly damaged, am I actually still alive?

I'm tired of being a bereaved mother, I'm tired of being without Harry. I just want him back. I don't care if he's close by, 'the other side of the veil', and that sometimes I can feel him and one day I might be with him again. *This is not enough!* I just need him physically here, now. I yearn for him and ache beyond words. I miss him to such an excruciating degree that I just come back to the fact that I don't think I can live on much longer without him. I have been trying, really trying to crawl up to some higher ground. Although there are moments when I can enjoy something fleetingly, the waves of pain soon roll in once more and the longing for him returns with such a vengeance that it's just too much to bear, again. I don't want to live like this. It really is beyond my tolerance to keep going and I feel resentful that I have to go on for everyone else. I am angry that this totally devastating loss has ruined my life. I shouldn't have had to witness my son's dead body, plan his funeral, make decisions about his ashes, read his postmortem report, watch his friends turn 25 when he never will.

Everyone else's lives go on and I realise, for the sake of the friendships I have left, I can't *just* talk about Harry. So, I try to show an interest in their lives, what their children are doing. It's hard sometimes to hear about matters which seem so trivial in comparison to what's happened to me and I see friends forgetting as they tell me. I understand. But it hurts. Everything hurts.

Sometimes I realise my honesty makes people uncomfortable. They probably don't want to know the extent of my wretchedness. I am quite open about the times when I don't want to live. I rationalise that, if I talk about it, I won't do anything about it, but it's probably hard to hear. To cheer them up, when I'm having a better day, I say I'll try to stay for a few years more. Sometimes I tell myself that each day I manage to get through brings me one day closer to being with Harry again. I have a distant notion that this is a very sad way of viewing life but it's really the best I can manage right now if I'm to stay.

I realise that I can't be the only grieving mother who has these thoughts. The feeling you don't want to live must be pretty common amongst bereaved parents. Later, I read a post in one of the more 'positive' Facebook groups that I'm a part of – it's from a mother who rather hesitantly asks if anyone else has ever felt suicidal. Within a few hours, there are over a hundred replies from mothers all saying yes. They say the pain, especially early on, makes it hard to continue living and that they just so desperately want to be with their dead child. Many, however, add that they eventually move past this and feel, whether they want to or not, that they have to stay for their other family members.

I wonder if the complete absence of fear of death you acquire when you've lost your child makes you bold to the possibility of leaving this life when the pain becomes so great – in a way that others might struggle to comprehend. My life no longer seems valuable in the way that it once did. There's no point now in thinking about a future and striving for happiness as I might have done before. In some ways, this is actually quite freeing, but in other ways, it's just horribly depressing. Probably a lot of us who have experienced this worst of all losses, when not at our very lowest, feel we are just biding our time, holding on to life very loosely.

Chapter 11

The Dark Night of the Soul

...to live is to suffer, to survive is to find meaning in the suffering.
If there is a purpose in life at all, there must be a purpose in
suffering and in dying. But no man can tell another what this
purpose is. Each must find out for himself...
Viktor E Frankl, *Man's Search for Meaning*

At the end of the summer, I realise that I must have actually
been doing better than I thought because now something
happens to make me see I am truly treading a tightrope that I
can be knocked off so very, very easily. I have been managing
the PTSD by rarely challenging myself and taking the view that
it will get better in time and that it's fine to only do what feels
comfortable until I'm ready. Now, all that changes.

One Sunday night, I'm drifting off to sleep, when the landline
rings. My heart starts racing. It's late. Only my parents use the
landline. I hear Anthony, still awake, answer. It's my mum. I
know it's not good.

It turns out she blacked out and was unconscious on the floor
for three hours before she pulled the cord in her assisted flat,
only to wait another four hours for the ambulance to arrive.
Half an hour before the ambulance finally arrives, she manages
to get to the phone and ring us.

Because he's still up and dressed, Anthony goes over to
Mum's flat. This leaves me in a similar situation to the night we
found Harry, also a Sunday. My heart is pounding, I feel sick,
I shake uncontrollably. My body is remembering the trauma. I
can't do this again, I just can't, I'm not strong enough. Lily is
with me and we try to calm each other. It will be alright, we say.

Once the ambulance arrives, Anthony comes back home and

takes me to the hospital and I spend the whole night in A&E with Mum whilst they run tests. My body and my brain are in meltdown, but I have to remain strong for Mum who is very frightened. By 6 a.m. she's on a ward. We are both exhausted and I go home to try to get some sleep, but my body is replicating what it did after we found Harry. I shake and hear my heart thumping out of my chest. I'm back on high alert.

There follows a week of being at the hospital for the majority of my day, sitting with Mum, anxious because I'm worried about her as well as anxious because of my PTSD response. Everything takes ages; I chase doctors or nurses for test results which take so long to come back and, confusingly, every doctor seems to give a different opinion as to why Mum collapsed. I feel like I'm in a new nightmare. She is moved from ward to ward until eventually, on a cardiac ward, she is in a room with one other woman who has her entire, very noisy, extended family with her most of the time. Worse still, she has a radio on loudly and continuously. Mum doesn't want to say anything, but I'm losing the plot and my mind by now. I realise the PTSD makes me hypersensitive to noise, smells, bright lights, people, everything really – not ideal when you're stuck in a hospital environment.

I can't bear to see Mum looking and feeling so frail but I am not really up to the job of supporting her as I once would have been. It's just too much. I feel rage towards my brother, who lives in France and hasn't come over to see her for over two years. I am beside myself with fury that I am not an only child but am expected to deal with the full responsibility of this situation as if I am. On top of the magnitude of everything I am going through.

At one point, the music from the radio of the woman in the next bed, in addition to the wait for several hours for some test results, tips me over. I'm really cracking now; it feels like I'm starting to have a breakdown. I have to get out. I run out of the ward and the building. Outside, I see a bus and consider stepping in front of it. I look at a tall concrete staircase, contemplate climbing it and then jumping off. I have no fear of my own death. I now really believe I could do it.

This is the very closest I have actively come to suicide. My unbearable life, my unrelenting grief, my traumatised being, the unfair sole responsibility for my mum, it's all become too much, too intolerable. 'God never gives you more than you can handle'? Well yes, actually, he does, and that's why people kill themselves. I certainly feel now that I have been given more than I can bear and I am raging. Not least, in the end, because being at a hospital, help would come quickly and I might be saved and put on the psychiatric ward. I'm trapped in a hell on earth and I badly want to leave.

But I don't. I hate myself for making it all about me. My poor mum, who I love so much – why can't I put aside my own feelings for hers? And I do try, I really do, but I am just so broken and damaged now and very, very angry. I have to somehow force myself back from the brink of a full-on breakdown. She needs me and so do Lily and Anthony.

Once Mum comes out of hospital, there are things to organise for her care and, for now, I visit her most days. It's just as well I haven't started working again. There's no conclusive diagnosis and she is naturally worried it will happen again, but the immediate crisis has passed. I now have to bring my physical and mental trauma response under control.

My fragility has terrified me. It didn't take much to push me dangerously close to the edge and I think perhaps I should get help. I contact a therapist who specialises in trauma and say I'm interested in meeting her for a session because I'm traumatised by my son's death. She asks me: 'When was it your son took his own life?' 'My son didn't kill himself' I say, taken aback. Not taken aback by the suicide bit – after all, I have just come close myself – but by the rather shocking assumption she has just made, by her crass insensitivity. It upsets me and I'm thrown. It doesn't bode well, and I wonder if I should go to see her after all.

In the end, I do go as she does EMDR, a therapy for PTSD that I want to try. But for some reason, it doesn't work for me, which is very disappointing. I continue for a few weeks, really hoping the sessions will make some difference, and they do help to a small degree but eventually I get upset by some heavy-handed observations she makes, along with a feeling that she can't really comprehend what I'm going through. I come to the conclusion that only other bereaved parents are going to fully 'get it'. I also think that being a coach means I perhaps see too much of the 'workings' of what a therapist may be trying to do and how their own belief systems can inevitably influence their viewpoint.

When I later have a conversation with other bereaved mothers about therapists, it transpires that quite a few say they didn't find the help they needed. Others had downright bad experiences and were shocked by the lack of sensitivity or understanding of how losing your child is truly the worst thing that can ever happen to a parent. I increasingly begin to think that further down the line, counselling or coaching bereaved mothers is something I could perhaps do. This starts to provide a faint glimmer of hope for potentially finding a purpose in my life again.

In the meantime, perhaps I am more capable than I realise of getting myself through this without professional help. One useful strategy the therapist does suggest is to get me to consider what I have in my 'basket of resources'. It appeals to me to make a list of everything that helps make my journey through this hell a little more bearable. I realise there is quite a lot, from writing to yoga, to herbal remedies. She also surprises me with her belief in the power of crystals and I rediscover my fascination with them. I find it comforting to hold them, their coolness, solidity and weight is soothing, and if it's true that they have healing benefits, then even better.

The Good Die Young

This is the truth of being a bereaved parent: People have asked me what's it like to live life with a deceased child because they 'just can't fathom'...Well, let me do my best to explain it in a way that can be understood. It's being dead but still being able to breathe, barely.
Unknown

My mum finds a quote attributed to the Greek historian Herodotus (c.484–425 BC): 'Whom the gods love die young', and I wonder, are people who die young distinctive or special in some way? Through my reading and from talking to other bereaved parents, I am starting to notice that those who don't have long lives appear to have certain character traits in common. They seem invariably to be kind, sensitive, 'old souls', wise beyond their years, often helping, and going out of their way to include, the underdog. Interestingly, they are also often described as unconventional, non-conformist or unique, either in their talents or personality or both. It seems there is no getting away from the fact that the vast majority of children and young people who die early, their age and cause of death being irrelevant, do appear to share certain characteristics. Of course, we consider Harry to be special – we are his family – but reading the many heartfelt comments in his 'memory book' highlights that others very much felt the same.

One sunny autumn day, Anthony and I are sitting in a park on a bench with a plaque dedicated to someone who has died aged 68. Not anywhere near as young as Harry but still relatively young to die these days. We now always seek out these inscribed benches during our walks.

On this particular October morning we sit overlooking the water. We look at the glorious shades of leaves in vibrant red, orange and gold, rustling in the gentle wind as we sit in the low sunlight, still warm for the time of year. I can appreciate moments of beauty like this, I say to Anthony, but is it really enough to make life worth continuing with? I ask him if he feels like the sadness is now firmly embedded within him and he wholeheartedly agrees. He certainly carries an air of sadness about him now but he doesn't touch the actual pain as often as I do. If I'm just sad, I consider it a better day. Later, though, when I say I feel that bereaved parents are rather like the living dead, he surprises me by saying this is exactly how he feels.

At Halloween, I find myself thinking differently about this occasion that 'celebrates' the dead. I have very happy memories of past Halloweens when Harry and Lily were young. Now, though, the idea that we dress our children up, decorate our houses with images of ghosts and ghouls and generally promote death as either something to be feared, or alternatively to be taken incredibly light-heartedly, strikes me as bizarre when you consider the pain involved in someone you love dying. But death is certainly no longer anything I fear, not now it has actually stopped at my door.

Sometimes, now that my entire brain seems to operate differently, strange, seemingly random memories come completely unbidden. One memory is of playing Cordelia in *King Lear* as a student. I remember how, perhaps oddly in hindsight, I really loved being 'dead'. I found it so relaxing and peaceful, like nothing mattered any more. Being carried on by the actor playing King Lear, letting my body go completely limp, felt very freeing. Then as I was put down on the stage, I lay there completely still, feeling strangely vulnerable, but not in a bad, exposing way. It was like I wasn't fully connected to my body, like I was separate from it, and I felt at peace with that. It's such a clear memory and I wonder now if I had a small glimpse of what it might actually feel like to be dead, free of all earthly concerns. Now I remember that King Lear dies from the grief of losing his child Cordelia. Shakespeare lost a son as well.

It was, of course, common to lose children with terrifying frequency in Shakespeare's time, or at any time up until the last century. Did the relative commonness of child loss make it easier to bear? I think sometimes, because of Harry's age, about the world wars, especially the first, and how so many young men didn't come back. Would you feel less alone in your pain knowing so many other sons didn't come back to their parents? Certainly, living in a time when it's unusual for your child to die before you do, bereaved parents today feel inextricably set apart from parents who have all their children living throughout their lives. It can feel very isolating. We will unconditionally love our dead children forever, just like those fortunate enough to have living children. We will still want to speak about them but we definitely don't want anyone's pity.

I realise, in some ways, I am quite fortunate in the support I've found. I speak to a woman who lost her child seven years ago and it sounds as if she has been very isolated in her grief. She hasn't read any books on child loss or even general bereavement and hasn't, it seems, found anything that might help her. Although she initially had some bereavement counselling, she didn't find it to be particularly beneficial and she's never heard of The Compassionate Friends. I'm shocked when she tells me that I'm the first bereaved mother she has ever spoken to. She must have felt – and must still feel – so very lonely in her loss and my heart goes out to her. This really makes me appreciate that I have people around me and that I've thankfully found various ways to support myself, that I am part of groups of other bereaved parents who share my experience, and that I derive a beneficial understanding of my situation from the books that I read.

However, grief must inevitably shape-shift as time goes by. Now, for me, it's still new and fresh and raw. But how will it be years from now? I suspect in these early stages that, although you can feel lonely because of the relative rarity of your experience, there are enough people around who want to support you. Therefore, true loneliness is usually kept at bay – for the moment. But what happens later when they become more used to your loss? From what I've read and heard, when you've been bereaved for years, you are more or less expected to put on a brave face and stop talking about your loved one. If that's the case, then surely a feeling of loneliness is likely to increase. I try to stop myself racing ahead and to just address what I'm facing now, but sometimes it's hard – you desperately hope it might somehow get better but then find you keep stumbling over so many 'what ifs'.

The nights draw in and I realise how spring and summer were easier to live through in some ways. The worst thing of all is that Sunday nights now feel more like the dark and cold Sunday night when we found Harry. The flashbacks come and I try to just go with them. I get out my winter coat and the memories of that night engulf me. I wore this coat over my pyjamas. Even though I must have worn it again afterwards, for some reason, now I can't bring myself to.

At nine months, I equate the length of time with that of carrying Harry in my womb. When you have a living child, you don't look back on this often once your child is grown. Now, though, I remember how I loved experiencing our growing bond, how amazing it was to grow a human. I had such a sense of who Harry was, his energy, how very alive he was wriggling about, how he calmed down as I stroked my stomach, how I talked to him and sang to him. I loved him so from the very start, before he even entered this world.

When he was born, he cried a lot, wanted to feed all the time and was a terrible sleeper (nothing changed there). After a very difficult birth and a blood transfusion, I was, albeit in a temporary way, quite traumatised. In a different time, neither of us would have survived. I remember thinking, *I will just have to take this one day at a time, just get through today.* Now his life here is over, that's what I find myself doing again. I take one day at a time.

Chapter 12

The Unbreakable Bond

The struggles are not fought and won, but faced again and again.
Progress is seen as the conflicts become less frequent, less intense,
of shorter duration, and easier to understand.
Linda Edelstein, *Maternal Bereavement*

Although several months have passed since I saw the early stages of Harry's bench installation, only now is it actually cemented into the ground and the plaque ready to be attached. We have a small low-key ceremony on a damp autumn afternoon. There's a lot of traffic and everyone is late. I try not to get stressed and upset. Fortunately, the man from the council says he can wait to put on the plaque. Eventually, Anthony reads a poem and some of the very moving comments from the memory book. When Anthony finishes, the man from the council seems to appear from nowhere and very rapidly puts on the plaque. I find I feel shocked as I see Harry's name and the dates of his birth and death and I start to cry. Everyone is talking to one another, so I am touched when Tom is immediately at my side to give me a hug. How can it possibly be that Harry has his name on a park bench, the very park he used to play in when he was a little boy? The dates look so wrong underneath the familiar name, especially the date of his death. Once again, my brain can't quite make sense of it all.

We go to the pub. I wonder how I will cope with this and if it will make me anxious. As it's at the end of our road, I know I can just leave at any point. In fact, because I'm surrounded by people who know what I must be feeling and who loved Harry, I'm actually fine and I enjoy talking to his friends and hearing stories about him.

I am relieved that Harry's friends don't appear likely to forget him as I had been beginning to fear. The bench was, of course, their idea and hopefully, in the coming months and years, they will visit it and use it as somewhere they can go to think of Harry. When I speak to them it's clear he is often in their thoughts, that they miss him and that his death has had a huge impact upon them. He has left a gap in their lives. He was very loved and I am so glad.

I am somehow surviving and doing my best to live a life with its current and very much ongoing restrictions of grief and PTSD. I'm being patient with myself, knowing the pain has to be gone through. However, I find I have a growing lack of patience when I hear someone, who really has a comparatively easy life, moaning about something I now consider trivial. I know I was most likely guilty of this in my 'before' life too, but now it makes me furious that people just don't know how fortunate they really are and how pointless it is to worry about things that are just so unimportant in the grand scheme of things.

I can often sense someone's relief at not being me, but I try not to think too much about how some people must pity me. Pity feels so patronising. Compassion, by contrast, feels kind and genuinely caring. I most definitely don't want to be pitied and I also don't want to be defined as a victim, even if in some ways I am. I'm told that my next-door neighbour hears me crying. I wish I hadn't been told this as it now inhibits me. I know it's healthy to cry in order to release some of the pain, even if I am heartily sick of doing so. In order to grieve freely, sometimes now, when I'm in the car and no one can hear me, I scream at the top of my lungs and sob loudly to release all the rage and hurt.

When I can, in the gaps between the still relentless misery of missing Harry, I try to consider the prospect of 'post-traumatic growth'. I read *Finding Meaning* by David Kessler and I realise that I need to find measurable ways to survive this. He says that loss is what happened to you but meaning is what you make happen. One day, walking back from Mum's, I have a precious moment of hope and unexpected, fleeting joy. It comes out of thinking about what I have to be grateful for – feeling the sun on my face on this bright winter's day, the invigorating cold air, that I have energy and more strength now, even that I'm alive and surviving. And best of all, I feel Harry with me and all his love, willing me on.

The Build-up to Christmas

Unless you have buried a child, you have no idea what a bad day really is.
Kelly Farley and David DiCola, *Grieving Dads: To the brink and back*

The Christmas period, I soon realise, is something the newly bereaved get through with great difficulty – particularly bereaved parents who have happy memories of Christmases with a child that is no longer here. It becomes something to dread, and the relentless and lengthy build-up to it taunts us. We also have Lily's twenty-first birthday on the horizon, a milestone in her life and one her brother won't be there for.

In November, we have a Compassionate Friends meeting that's focused entirely on how to survive Christmas and I am keen to know how this is to be done. I have been imagining that Christmas is simply ruined forever but it seems that, for some at least, by the third Christmas you may start to find some small enjoyment in certain aspects of it. I am so encouraged by this. For me, there are some in our group who give me much-needed hope that it can get better. Obviously, the grief is ongoing forever but I just need to know that the intensity of suffering may diminish. I am frankly desperate to believe all this is somehow going to get easier because the alternative is just too intolerable to contemplate. I, therefore, gravitate to the people further down the line than I am, who might shine a light for me to follow to the higher ground.

We are warned at the meeting, those of us who have yet to experience Christmas in the new world, that Christmas cards can be upsetting. I rather dismiss this at the time but then we start receiving some where Harry is airbrushed out. It's hard enough seeing our three names where we used to see four, but when Harry isn't even mentioned, it rather takes my breath away. Some people do include him, though – they either say 'Thinking of you at this difficult time' or 'Remembering Harry', and I am so grateful for this acknowledgement. Then, however, there are the cards that are absent. Many people don't send cards any more and that's fine, but others have sent one every year up to now. It seems extraordinary that they have chosen this year to be silent. As I now know, only too well by this stage, there are so many ways to feel hurt by the behaviour of others when you're a bereaved parent.

The Unbreakable Bond

I could only be grateful when I realised that I would rather have known you for a moment than never at all. I would rather endure this inexplicable pain of outliving you than never have seen your face, spoken your name.
Vicki Harrison

At the beginning of December, I have a long-awaited reading with the medium Claire Broad, who has just published a book called *What the Dead Are Dying to Teach Us*. I feel as if I know her and I like her immediately as she opens her front door to me. I hope I won't be disappointed. Apart from a couple of things, the vast majority of what she tells me is very accurate and some of the session is frankly astonishing.

I feel Harry with us, without any doubt at all. He comes through so clearly and Claire is amazed by the things he tells and shows her. He comes out with some incredibly wise observations and I am so pleased to have this connection with him. Yet again, I'm told that he didn't need to be here for long, he'd done all he needed to do and that it was his time to go. And like the other mediums, Claire tells me how very strong our bond is and that he's with me all the time, guiding me. She says he's incredibly protective of me and that love shines out of him. I get shivers when Harry tells her of the quite obscure things that I've been reading about, which she couldn't possibly know and, in fact, I end up explaining to her. He also tells her I'm writing and that I'm going to help people as a result of what's happened to me. He tells her so many things she couldn't have known that it's truly remarkable.

Claire makes me laugh by saying although she likes telling people that their dead grandmother likes the red dress they've just bought, she prefers the kind of reading we're getting with Harry as it has such depth. The one-hour session goes on for over two. It really is an extraordinary reading. Claire reminds me to use what Harry is communicating via her, and in the other readings I have had, as validation of what I already know in my heart and says that this can potentially help me as I move through my grief.

Aside from constantly referencing how our souls are strongly connected, what gives me immeasurable comfort is Harry telling Claire that had he still been alive, he would be doing his own thing, living his own life, but now he is with me all the time. Amazingly, this is a conversation I 'imagined' having with Harry on the beach earlier in the year. She reassures me that he is absolutely fine where he is and that our relationship is continuing in a way that it couldn't have done if he was still here. Part of his purpose now, as well as his own soul growth, is to help and guide me. Harry is a living energy.

I have a week or so when my world completely shifts. This is the best I've felt since Harry died. I am delighted – it's not as bad as I thought, I will survive after all! I can go forward and still have Harry, just in a different way; I'm still connected to him and know he's with me all the time. I *feel* him, I know he's there! Love conquers all, it's true. I'm going to be okay; I just have to hold on tight to this feeling, not let it slip through my fingers.

And then I get ill. It's nothing serious, just a rather nasty virus involving a very bad headache and painful sinuses. In all, it takes about ten days before I start to feel better. It has not escaped my notice that I've been pretty healthy since Harry died. Knowing what grief and stress can do to the body, that's been quite surprising to me. I put my lack of any illness down to the possibility that it might be because I'm expressing my grief freely and therefore it's not 'stuck' in my body. At least, I hope that might be the case. So why now, when I'm actually feeling the best I've felt, have I succumbed to a really horrible virus? I wonder if perhaps my improved emotional state has allowed space for physical stuff to come forward and be released in some way. I'm aware that I always seem to need an explanation for why something happens, to make sense of everything. Maybe things don't always happen for a particular reason – or maybe it doesn't always matter.

Anyway, along with the dip in my physical health, I, unfortunately, find my emotional health starting to plummet too. I really don't want to lose my grip again. I have to cancel seeing friends and I don't feel up to going out for walks, both so necessary for me. It's such a shame as I had really been looking for ways to make Christmas without Harry both bearable and meaningful.

Although I still feel unable to part with many of Harry's possessions, we make the decision to give away several pairs of his shoes and a coat to a homeless organisation. I think this is what Harry would want and I hope he would be pleased with me for letting some of his things go to be made good use of. I also decide to only give Christmas presents that are related to him. Tree decorations with his name on, candles that say 'A Beautiful Soul Is Never Forgotten', stones with 'Harry' engraved in them and a mini Christmas tree which has the initial H on top instead of a star. I print a poem for Mum and frame it and gather photos of the two of them and frame these too. She will cry as she opens them. We fill a supermarket trolley with his favourite food and donate it all to the homeless. I suggest we all wear one of his shirts on Christmas Day as another way to honour him, to still have him with us in some way.

All this I plan before I get ill and it keeps me buoyed up, but then I feel myself slipping. I'm not fully recovered but I feel a lot better physically by Christmas Day. However, in my somewhat debilitated state, I have to face the fact that Christmas without Harry cannot ever be made better, despite my attempts. I just need to get through it. I realise it will be difficult for all of us, not just me.

The day itself is very painful, like walking on broken glass. We go through some of the motions of a normal Christmas but as we sit down to lunch, none of us can speak. By the late afternoon, I can take no more, I'm defeated. I walk upstairs and climb into bed. I slide down under the cool murky greyness as I head back to the bottom of the sea.

It is too hard to live this blighted life, I'm too weak and I hate myself for it. I've really tried but I just can't any more. Over the next few days, I either can't get out of bed or if I do, I find myself soon getting back into it. The torment is colossal, my tears unending. I can't feel Harry close to me any more. Where is he? I can't find him. He's abandoned me all over again. I'm angry with him. I decide to give up. I want to die. It will be better for all of us.

But I don't die and now it's New Year and I find I feel absolute panic. I am delirious with images of a vulnerable and scared little blond boy left on a station platform as we pull out on an unstoppable train, leaving him behind forever in the year just gone, failing to take him forward with us into the future, into the coming year. And it feels just unbearable.

Chapter 13

The Abyss Again

I measure every grief I meet
With analytic eyes
I wonder if it weighs like mine
Or has an easier size
I wonder if it hurts to live
Or if they have to try
And whether, could they choose between,
They would not rather die.
Emily Dickinson

I am well and truly back in the abyss now and I don't know if I'm going to find my way out this time. I stay there, paralysed, not even attempting to move. It's almost comfortable in the stillness of giving up, but not quite, because you can't ever really feel comfortable when you're waiting for the next wave of excruciating agony. Sometimes, it feels like I'm in a soft and warm cocoon and that, if I keep very still, I won't have to feel the pain any more. But if I move, the sharp blades and shiny razors that surround my safe cocoon will cut me, often deeply and to the bone.

Time moves very slowly, and I can do nothing but cry and ruminate, simmering in my suffocating grief. However, by the middle of January, I am starting to claw my way up yet again, to crawl out of this life-sucking grief coma I've been in. The weather is awful but still, getting out and walking helps to save me. I read again, yet more books on grief and on spirituality, and they help too. I do guided meditations and grief yoga. I try, I really try, and it's incredibly hard and the effort is exhausting. Every so often, I slide down to the bottom again and stay there for a bit but then pull myself up once more so that I can see that chink of light.

For weeks now, I have pretty much been a hermit and I know some people have become worried about me. Back at the beginning of December, an old client contacts me asking for an appointment and I book her in for the end of January as it feels safely far away in the future. I could cancel her, but I know I have to start working again soon, not least for financial reasons. I realise that the very last time I held a consultation, sitting on the same chair, asking the same questions, writing in the same notebook, Harry would have been living his very last hours on this earth.

In the end, the consultation itself is fine but afterwards, I feel such a sense of despondency and overwhelming sadness because it feels as if I've just stepped back in time, reverting to something I did in my old life. I'd give anything to go back to that old life that had Harry in it, alive on earth. But I can't. So, how can I just go back to doing the same thing I used to do before when I'm now an entirely different person, so very profoundly altered?

I have to try to find a way forward. I decide it's time to make some changes. I remove from my website the statement about not taking on new clients. I make changes to some of the wording, which now rather grates on me with its positive message of a life full of health, vitality and wellbeing, and I add grief coaching to my services. I decide this is the direction I want to go in now, how I think I may be able to galvanise my own grief into something meaningful. I did a required module on bereavement in my training to be a wellbeing coach and obviously, I'm only too familiar with what it's like to grieve. I've also read extensively. I'm not ready to start yet and I will undertake some additional training, but putting it out there seems to acknowledge and encompass the new aspects of myself and all I've learnt.

Could this really be a way to use the terrible thing that has happened to me? Could I eventually offer a service for other bereaved people, supporting their emotional and physical health and their wellbeing? My own experience of therapy and counselling didn't help me much and, although some find it useful, I know many don't. Perhaps I can offer a different way. After all, who can possibly understand a bereaved mother better than another bereaved mother?

I'm aware that I'm still considered to be early on in my 'grief journey', but it's an idea and it gives me a much-needed sense of purpose, a way to potentially use the skills I already had and the ones I've unfortunately had to gain. I read that you can be in pain yourself but still sit with someone else's, and I find this to be encouraging. This could be my post-traumatic growth. I really want to try to alchemise my grief into something that can honour Harry and benefit others.

The reality is, though, I now have to build up my practice pretty much from scratch, having had to let all my existing clients go when Harry died. I find I'm more philosophical about this than I was. It's okay that it will build slowly. I'm still in the early stages of my healing and it wouldn't be good for me to take on too much at this stage.

One afternoon, I get a call from a young man who says he's a musician in his mid-twenties and that he's suffering from insomnia caused by his nocturnal lifestyle. He wants to make changes as it's increasingly affecting his health and wellbeing. I'm not sure how I feel – is this a chance to help someone with similar issues and of a similar age to Harry who's also a musician? To alert him to the potentially serious consequences upon health of not sleeping properly and not eating well? Or is it just going to be incredibly triggering, making me feel that I failed to help my own son with his diet and lifestyle despite my best efforts? In the end, I have no need to feel any angst over it – he cancels ten minutes before he's due for his consultation. I am both annoyed and relieved.

The Broken Heart

A broken heart is not just a broken heart.
It is an instrument of coherence.
The break permits the awakening...
Broken, but for the first time in truth...
Not knowing how, we stumble at first.
Wishing for the grief to go away so we can go back to sleep...
Life without any grief provides a comfortable bed that carries no evolution.
And yes, you may not care about evolution, you and I would definitely choose to have our people back, but our world was not made this way...
This is why your mission should be to stay in the intelligence of grief and build not only sand castles but learn how to make it outside of grief's gravity.
Christina Rasmussen

I have read, and I was also told by Claire Broad, that a loss of this nature can open your heart and make you more compassionate to the suffering of others. I do feel my heart has been opened, or rather it was wrenched open in a way I'd rather it hadn't been. I feel I have been awakened to the bigger picture, to questioning life, death, our purpose for being here. However, I wonder about being more compassionate as, until this point, I'm not sure my experience has necessarily brought to the fore compassion, patience and tolerance. I think in some ways I've actually become more intolerant of those who I now perceive as having minor problems, namely anyone who hasn't had a significant bereavement or trauma. And sometimes I'm just too blinded by my own all-absorbing pain and loss to feel as much compassion for others as I would like.

However, as I start to see more clients, I find my patience isn't as tested as I had feared by people whose experiences aren't as bad as my own. I find I can put myself aside and just simply think of what I can do to help them, though often after being focused wholly on someone else for an hour or so, I come crashing back to the heartbreaking reality of my own life.

The Quest for Answers

Spirituality assists you in making sense of the world and who you are. It connects you with the profoundly powerful and divine force of the Universe.
James Van Praagh, *Adventures of the Soul*

In his book *Companioning the Bereaved*, Alan Wolfelt says that loss calls out for a new search for meaning and that it is the spiritual dimension of grief that allows us to go on living. Throughout all these months since Harry's death, I have had an overriding need to make sense of why he died. The fact is we will never know for sure what happens after death until we die ourselves, but I do feel I have found some answers that give me some semblance of peace. A year ago, I would have said, if asked, that I believed in a power higher than myself and that I was open to the idea that we carry on in some way after death, but it wasn't something I gave a huge amount of thought to. The pivotal moment of change in my beliefs was undoubtedly seeing Harry's dead physical body and knowing, with absolute certainty, that he was no longer in it. His essence wasn't gone; it was simply somewhere else.

Being told very pragmatically by the first medium that it was Harry's time to go, that he was never going to be here for long and that he'd done all he had to do in this lifetime, just seemed to make such sense to me and confirmed what I already knew in my soul. The subsequent sessions with mediums, and the books I've read, endorse my developing beliefs about life after death. I'm fortunate that all three mediums I consulted were very good ones and they notably crossed over a lot in what they told me which, although maybe not actual proof, does provide at least some sort of cumulative evidence that what they said may be true.

I have now read a great deal about reincarnation, soul groups, soul agreements and pre-life planning. The latter being where your soul agrees to take on certain 'lessons' during a lifetime (which may be shared with others from your soul group) in order to evolve. There is free will, but there are a number of circumstances that, once agreed upon, will happen. There may be a time frame for how long a life will be, as perhaps there was for Harry. From the perspective of spirit, all life here is short and temporary, a place we come to have experiences which provide opportunity for immeasurable growth, taking us to greater levels of understanding and helping our souls to mature and evolve.

I read that the grief of child loss is the most transformative type of loss anyone on the planet can experience and carries with it the most potential for soul growth. If this is true and I 'agreed' to this prior to coming here, then I've clearly now changed my mind and have no idea what my soul was thinking of, if this is what it 'planned'. Regardless of whether this is the case or not, these concepts are, at the very least, interesting to explore, though of course, I would rather not be in a position where I need to do so.

The fact is, I live in a different world now, one which makes me feel brave to all possibilities and open to entertaining any number of ideas regarding why Harry died young, why we're here, why I am having to go through this experience. And I think I've always felt, even before Harry died, that death isn't the end and that there is definitely something more. It's just that I didn't need to think about it very much before…

The signs and dreams that I, and others, think we have received from Harry, along with the strong sense that he is with me, reinforce my beliefs. I fluctuate between caring and not caring about whether anyone thinks I'm delusional because of what's happened to me, but generally, this is just what I believe now – that Harry lives on in a different way, that he's fine, he's close by and that, one day, I will be reunited with him. In the meantime, our bond continues.

On reflection, I'm glad that, aside from the early weeks when I was in far too much shock to write, I have pretty much written about my grief in real time. I think now that this is important to me for seeing how I was shaped, not just by events at the time they occurred, but by all that I've learnt along the way, through my reading, by feeling Harry's presence, and by the visits to mediums. If, for example, I was only now starting to write, I would inevitably impose my current perspective, with all my accumulated new beliefs, onto my experiences over the past year. It's certainly difficult to know if we ever see past events as they actually were; everyone's truth is different, but I guess this becomes even more of an issue the later you leave writing about something.

Chapter 14

Survival

When you've lived through an unexpected or out of order death, your heart has, by definition, already been pushed too far. Your heart has been pushed beyond the limits of what most people will ever have to endure. I think it's brave that you get up in the morning even though your soul is weary and your bones ache for a rest. I think it's brave that you keep on living even though you don't know how to anymore. I think it's brave that you push away the waves rolling in every day and you decide to fight. I know there are days when you feel like giving up but I think it's brave that you never do.
Lana Rafaela

I am an entirely different person now. It's as if my soul has overflowed from the tiny world it once inhabited and expanded out into something unbound and limitless. There is no going back. I have no choice but to move forward because my shattered pieces don't fit together in the way they did before, and they're never going to. I have seen things I can't unsee. I've gone to a core of pain I didn't realise existed. I now know things I didn't know before; my eyes have been forced open to see that there is more to life than I had realised, even if I don't fully understand it yet, and maybe never will. Perhaps you only get to glimpse this bigger picture if something life-changing happens to you, forcibly cracking apart everything you thought you knew and held to be true.

Reflection on the First Year
As the first anniversary of Harry's death approaches, I start to get an increase in flashbacks again and to relive some of the trauma.

I look back in amazement at what we have been through. It feels as if you defy the absolute impossible when you continue to live on when your child has died. I still wonder how I have survived the heart-stopping shock of Harry's death, how I've managed to withstand such a fierce agony which has so often felt completely beyond human endurance. But I'm still here and I am surviving, though I'm weary of constantly fighting for that survival. However, I've always understood that the only way is through. I have never shied away from the searing pain and that ultimately must surely be helping me towards some sort of healing.

I read that grieving the loss of your child starts the day you lose them and ends the day you join them. I know in my heart that this is going to be true. The fallout from the death of your child is, unfortunately, a life sentence and this is hardly surprising – losing your child is the most shocking trauma a human being can endure. Everything is charged with the potential for reminder and this means life always seems to be tinged with a sadness that there is just no getting away from. My love for Harry and my grief at not having him in this world will never end. I imagine I will ache for Harry until I die. I will just hopefully become more and more accustomed to that ache, especially as I get beyond the first year.

I start to reflect on any progress I have made. Certainly, the physical symptoms of shock and trauma aren't present on a daily basis any more but, as I experienced when my mum collapsed, they are there lurking in the background, ready to remember their imprint. I am starting to do more of the things I once took for granted. I have been able, albeit still to a limited degree, to sit in cafes again and go to the shops. I have been to the theatre without excessive anxiety, though I did cry silently as I sat in the auditorium looking at the people around me. People who looked like they were leading enviably normal, tolerable lives with enviably normal, tolerable levels of pain; my own level of pain most likely to be something they couldn't even begin to comprehend and luckily will probably never have to.

That I am working again is certainly progress. I can focus on someone else's problems and genuinely want to help them, which only a few months previously I wasn't sure I could ever do again. I speculate that if you told them I had lost my son only 11 months ago, they would be amazed. I can put my pain aside for the time I am with them. I find that I still like helping people and I can now, just for a short while, operate as if I'm a normal person. I can smile and even appear upbeat when required. I think Harry would be pleased to see my modest progression.

The First Anniversary

You will find a way to bear the unbearable by going forward into the unknown. You do not have to know how to survive right now to succeed at doing so in the future.
Nisha Zenoff, *The Unspeakable Loss*

I wake early on this first anniversary of my child's death and I feel okay. I have had a dream where I've been laughing uncontrollably, proper, side-aching belly laughing, and I seem somehow to have carried this feeling of joy and lightness into my waking state. Was Harry in the dream laughing with me? I can't remember, but it feels like he might have been. Anyway, surprisingly, I don't feel as bad as anticipated. I turn on my phone and there are already several text messages. This helps, along with the cards and flowers we've been sent. I have never once stopped appreciating the kindness, compassion and love we have received during this harrowing year.

Anthony went out with Harry's friends last night but, for me, it doesn't feel right to do much. We put white roses around Harry's plaque in the garden and we light a candle by it. We think he died around 2 p.m. so at that time Anthony and I head up to his bench in the park and tie two white roses either side of the plaque. It feels like this represents us, his mum and dad, close and either side of him, protecting him with our immeasurable and never-ending love.

We go back home and take a candle up to his bedroom and we sit there and listen to his music on Spotify. Finally, I can listen to his music. Yes, I feel sad, but it's bittersweet sadness today and not pure, blazing, agonising torture. I find myself remembering specific songs being composed in this very room. I see Harry's tall slim body, his beautiful fine-boned pale face and his long artistic fingers, as he bends over his keyboard and mixing board, deep in concentration. Playing each phrase over and over, and being a perfectionist, never feeling he got it quite right. I wish he'd realised he was so talented, and I wish we'd told him more.

We decide to sort out some of his paperwork, papers that we can bear to part with, that we won't have any sentimental attachment to. In amongst some of these papers, however, we discover a Valentine's card from his first girlfriend. It's very touching and Anthony is crying as he reads it out to me. She says it's their fourth Valentine's Day together and she loves him very much but, as they're not even 20 yet, they probably won't get married as they've met so early in their lives. But she hopes to be his best friend forever and that in their twenties, they will still sit on beanbags watching YouTube videos together, laughing their heads off. This did in fact more or less happen – they remained friends and every so often would spend time together, possibly doing exactly that.

I clear out a cardboard box full of books that Harry had taken to his flat and put them back onto his shelves. I take out his fairy lights – the ones that were on when we found him – and put them up over the mantlepiece and turn them on. I find a small light projector I remember him using, but I can't work out how to use it. I mentally ask him how it works and wondrously

I manage to turn it on, laughing at the unexpected sounds of seagulls and the sea, as well as the lovely kaleidoscope of patterns that appear on the ceiling and look quite magical. It occurs to me that Harry inherited my romantic and aesthetic sensibility, and I hadn't really realised it before. I feel him with me and I am pleased I've brought his room back to life a little. It's getting dark, I've nearly done it. I've nearly survived a full year without my darling son and the pain hasn't been so great today. Love can override everything, if I can let it.

There is a complication for us with the anniversary in that the day Harry actually died, we remained in blissful ignorance. The day after is the day we found him and the day our lives changed forever and so is really just as significant. Having got through the actual anniversary relatively unscathed, I wake the next morning with a sense of dread about reliving in vivid detail the trauma of discovering that Harry was dead. That inexpungible memory of the horrifying call with Anthony telling me and changing my life in an instant. The frozen disbelief I felt, the startling fear, the terrifying helplessness of not having a car to get to Harry. The torturous, seemingly endless journey and the running up the stairs with legs that barely carried me, seeing him lying there, still and icy like marble, the emotionless, compassionless emergency services not acknowledging our distress and trauma. Just the ultimate, previously unknowable nightmare that no parent should have to endure, ever, ever, ever.

But we did endure it, and we still do. I distract myself by cleaning the house, planting the beautiful jasmine we have been given that will now always flower for Harry at this time of year, and by looking for a holiday, something for us to look forward to. But it's still there, the impending sense of doom that at 5.30 p.m., literally as the darkness descends, I will remember and that it will seem like it's happening all over again, embedded as it is now in the very cells of my body. I catch my breath as the panic rises and the tears come, tears that have been shed nearly every single day for a year. How is that even possible? I'm trying hard not to spiral. Once today is over, I can perhaps breathe again. Can I? I just don't know, it's all so hard to predict. I thought yesterday, the first anniversary, would be possibly the worst of all the occasions but actually it wasn't and Christmas and New Year felt infinitely worse. Going forward now into the second year, I wonder how it will feel, having done everything once. I'm hoping, if I don't have too many expectations, that it won't be as bad, that the second year may be easier because the longer you're without something, the more used to it you become. That surely should mean a reduction in the intensity of suffering, albeit not the grief itself. But then there is the sad fact that the length of time without Harry will only increase; it'll be longer since I saw his beautiful face, heard his voice or received one of his heart-melting hugs. I desperately need to believe that I won't always be in this amount of pain, but what if it's true that with a sudden death, the first year is just about dealing with the shock and that it's only when you get into the second year that you start to properly grieve? My heart sinks like a stone at this prospect. But in the end, if I've learnt anything, it's that the grieving process is very individual and unpredictable, and that there is no timeline for it. I just have to accept where I am at each moment. And continue to strive for hope.

I survive the day somehow, touching the trauma of remembering the same day exactly a year ago, and then stepping back for a bit. A dance I have done now for the past 12 months.

I have survived a whole year.

I didn't die of a broken heart or take my own life.

It seems I live on, without my boy.

The love between a mother and child is fierce and powerful,

but the love between a bereaved mother and her child is undoubtedly the most fierce and powerful of all.

And nothing can ever diminish that love, not even death.

When you are reduced to nothing but soul, you radiate an extraordinary power.

When you experience searing loss and your heart continues beating, there is strength in that.

When pain whispers the hurtful lies and giving up and succumbing sounds like the best plan, find that strength, find that hope that is greater and that love that is deeper than any amount of pain, then cling to it

AND DON'T YOU DARE LET GO.

Lexi Behrndt

Part Two

How to Support the Grieving Process

Introduction

The Reality of Grief, Survival and Hope

Although the world is full of suffering, it is also full of overcoming it.
Helen Keller

There is much suffering in life that we can overcome, but overcoming suffering is not the same as overcoming grief. I've come to believe that it's possible eventually to accommodate grief within your life and that the suffering associated with your loss can lessen with time. However, I also think you have to take active steps towards easing some of that suffering.

Grief is a part of life that few will be able to avoid, though thankfully the death of a child is not an experience everybody will face. Some people cope with loss better than others. This may be because the death of a loved one is expected and a long life has been lived. And some people just have a certain natural, or possibly worked-for, resilience. Others struggle and get stuck in their grief; the pain of their loss seemingly insurmountable. This is often referred to as 'complicated' or 'prolonged' grief and can often be seen with parents who have lost their child to a sudden, unexpected death.

I think it's likely that who you were before you were bereaved may influence your experience of grief too. As someone who has always been very sensitive and emotional, and felt things deeply, this perhaps, unfortunately, makes my grieving process extra painful and my low points particularly low. On the other hand, I have a strong capacity for hope, a desire to find meaning in my life again and a belief in life after death. This provides a certain counterbalance. I am determined to find joy when I can, in spite of what has happened to me, and sometimes I do.

In addition, my job as a nutritional therapist and wellbeing coach equips me with certain skills which I use to assist me as I navigate through my life after the death of my son. It now feels like the natural next step to share these with those of you who may be going through a similar experience, as well as suggesting other methods of support I have acquired along the way. Not everything will be right for you – we all grieve differently – but I offer these ideas in the hope that they might make this difficult path just a little easier.

One day you will tell your story of how you overcame what you went through and it will be someone else's survival guide.
Brené Brown

From the very beginning, I found I was motivated by a desperation to find anything that might help relieve some of my physical and emotional suffering. For many people, their GP is the first port of call, where medication and referral to a bereavement counsellor may be offered. I didn't take this route as I had a friend who ran our local bereavement service and, because of my background in nutritional medicine, I knew of natural and effective alternatives to sleeping pills, antidepressants and anti-anxiety medication.

The brutal truth is that the pain of grief cannot be avoided, nor should it be. The protective early stage of denial can help pace out the loss but, in the end, it is something you have to go through rather than around. It is undoubtedly painful beyond anything I have ever experienced. Excruciating as it is, it can be more damaging in the long term to avoid facing grief head on, and they do say 'Those who grieve well, live well' (an annoying quote when you've had a significant loss but I think it's probably true). You may find you are frequently told how brave and strong you are. You may not feel this is true – but you are because you have to be.

It's important to remember that grief isn't a problem that

needs to be solved. I am, by nature, someone who wants to fix things and find solutions. Often those around us try to do the same in an attempt to make us feel better. But grief is not a physical illness or a mental health issue, though both may be implicated as collateral, and there is nothing 'wrong' with you as such. Your pain is a natural reaction to having loved someone deeply and now having to adapt to their absence. We may feel we would do anything to be out of pain as soon as possible but, frustratingly, that's not how it works. Your grief needs supporting, not solving, and hopefully, some of the ideas in this part of the book might just do that – offer support, rather than a solution.

After the initial stages when you can feel quite paralysed at times, I think it can certainly help to see grief as an active rather than passive process. I know only too well that sometimes you can't help but sink down to rock bottom, seemingly prevented from moving by an overwhelming blanket of despair. But when you rise up again, either because you've determinedly pulled yourself up or because eventually you just seem to resurface for air, the following resources might be helpful in easing some of your suffering. They may also aid an understanding of the process of bereavement and trauma. Sadly, there is no magic wand for grief. Different things will help different people. Don't stick with something if it doesn't feel right for you. Cut your losses and try something else.

Always ask yourself, whether it's trying out a therapist or it's dealing with people, places and events: 'Does this help me, or does this hinder me?' At the very least, let grief liberate you from feeling you have to do things out of duty because you feel committed or to please somebody else. Being able to opt out of things you don't want to do without feeling guilty is one of the very few benefits of grieving.

Whilst I advocate finding ways to help yourself during

grief, there will be times when you just need to sit with it and do nothing. You have to allow yourself to be where you are. Sometimes it's about being, not doing. Follow your instincts on whether 'being' or 'doing' will serve you best for where you are in your healing. I have discovered there is much to learn between the pain and the seeking of peace, and it seems that allowing yourself to fully feel the pain when it rolls in can ultimately help with healing.

And finally, a broken heart is an open heart, and hope is everything. Hope is your fuel; it can empower and motivate, if you're able to let it do so. Look for little glimmers of it. Your life will never be the same now but, whoever you have lost, make them proud of you for surviving and of what you go on to do with the rest of your life.

Chapter 1

The Body's Response to Grief, Shock and Trauma

I was amazed at the very extreme response my body had to the trauma of my son's sudden death. It reacted with violent shaking, a racing heart, a speeded-up metabolism, nausea, insomnia, a gnawing in the stomach and constantly catching my breath. All these symptoms were felt with great intensity and were ongoing for quite some time, which was both startling and overwhelming. This is shock. The nervous system goes into overdrive and the stress hormones, adrenaline and cortisol, are released as part of the fight-or-flight response because the body thinks it's in danger. Shock is fundamentally a protective mechanism and it stops you from having to deal with the full impact of the emotional trauma you're experiencing. The physical symptoms can temporarily distract from this, at least some of the time. Studies have shown that infants with separation anxiety display increased cortisol levels. Researchers have made links between this attachment theory and the grief response – when separation or death occurs, then depression, anxiety, sleep loss and nervous system arousal are typical. Grief and trauma can be experienced separately or together, depending on the circumstances, but the physical responses to bereavement have many similarities to trauma anyway.

It is common after a significant loss to feel real physical pain in your heart and, of course, broken heart syndrome is an actual thing. In fact, it is now becoming recognised as a very real medical issue. Apparently, scans can show that the heart of someone with broken heart syndrome can look identical to the heart of someone who has heart disease. However, in the case of broken heart syndrome, the damage can go as quickly as it came, if the grief is effectively addressed.

Not everyone experiences an extreme physical response to loss and trauma but, like me, there are many that do. There may be times when you think your body won't survive the symptoms you experience. At certain points in early grief, I didn't think I could possibly live one more day without sleep, without being able to eat, with a heart that was continually thumping out of my chest and legs that seemed unable to hold me up. But I did. Further down the line, there may be panic attacks, crippling fatigue, breathlessness, brain fog and, of course, endless exhausting bouts of crying – and still, incredibly, you will find that you somehow survive.

Before this happened to me, I had no idea that grief could be such a physical thing, so visceral. It can put tremendous strain on your body in all manner of ways, including potentially suppressing immunity and digestion. The stress of grief can increase inflammation in the body, so it's very important to address any symptoms that might present themselves as soon as you can. Studies have shown that grief has the potential to very seriously affect your health. This has unfortunately proved to be the case with some of the bereaved parents I know. Research has shown that the likelihood of bereaved spouses having a sudden cardiac death rises significantly in the six months following a death, and traumatic grief symptoms can unfortunately precede illnesses such as cancer.

'Grief Brain'

This can be a frightening aspect of grief, affecting you both physically and mentally. Both trauma and grief can interfere with our ability to think clearly. You can find yourself forgetting arrangements you've made and completely erasing conversations you've had (probably to the annoyance of those around you!). I've always made lists and it was just as well I was in the habit of doing so, because I certainly needed them more than ever during the initial stages of grief.

At first, you may put any brain symptoms down to lack of sleep – but it's not just that. The stress from the trauma has flooded your body with cortisol. As a result, you feel foggy, confused, can't concentrate, can't think straight. It's known that emotional traumatic brain 'injury' following the death of a child or loved one can lead to definitive changes in brain function.

In her book *It's OK That You're Not OK*, Megan Devine writes that if you imagine you have 100 units of brain-power for each day, then around 99 of these energy units are now taken up by grief, trauma, sadness and so on. This leaves just one unit for normal daily activities. It's not surprising then that you're exhausted and can't do the simple tasks you used to take for granted. Your brain is doing the best it can do to survive and function under very challenging circumstances.

A traumatised brain is working extra hard and is generally overactive. In fact, many trauma survivors actually develop an enlarged amygdala – the part of the limbic system within the brain that's responsible for emotions, survival instinct and memory – leading to an ongoing over-triggered fight-or-flight response and a state of hyper-vigilance. Crucially, the brain also fails to perceive whether something happened in the past or is actually happening in the present. Sometimes it will relive the trauma in flashbacks, recreating the traumatic event(s). A traumatised brain is always on high alert and works much harder than a non-traumatised brain to keep up with everyday situations. No wonder it's exhausting! That's why it's important to try to break this pattern if you can.

Fundamentally, a good place to start is by just giving yourself permission to rest. Don't push yourself to do anything when it all feels too much – postpone visitors if they're going to drain you, delegate shopping to someone else, don't bother with housework. Simple breathing exercises may sound basic but they can be very effective for calming the nervous system. Your poor brain is just trying to protect you in the best way it can. Recognise this, acknowledge what you've been through, look after yourself and get help if you need to. You will find further suggestions outlined in the latter part of Chapter 2 in the section entitled 'Other Therapies'.

The good news is it can improve. My brain, whilst still traumatised to some degree, is functioning a lot better than it was. Some of that is down to time and the initial shock passing. However, various other things have helped heal my brain, including eating well, taking supplements that specifically support the brain and the nervous system, plus getting sufficient sleep and gentle exercise.

We can't do anything to change what has happened to us, but we can take measures to try to minimise some of the physical damage. I say that knowing full well that whatever might have seemed important before your loss may no longer feel like a priority. Looking after your health and wellbeing might not seem to matter very much initially. This is hardly surprising.

Eventually, the more extreme physical symptoms should pass, but in the very early stages of grief, all you can really do is try to eat whatever you feel you can manage and not worry too much about whether it's healthy or not. Limit coffee as your adrenal glands and nervous system will already be stimulated and working overtime. Alcohol is generally best avoided as it can disrupt sleep which you will need more than ever, as sleep is when the body does its repair work. Sleep is also when you can start to process what has happened to you emotionally.

Eating

If you're lucky, some kind friends and neighbours may bring you meals in the first few days or weeks. If anyone offers to do this, it's a very good idea to accept. You probably won't feel like making meals initially, or shopping, so these are the best ways people can support you to begin with. I know early in bereavement I couldn't eat very much at all, let alone cook, but when someone made a meal, I felt (relatively) better physically and emotionally after eating it. Blood sugar balance is important for mood and you don't want to feel worse than you need to, so it's vital not to go too long without eating. Stress uses up nutrients – and grief, as we're only too aware, is very stressful.

Sooner or later, you will need to feed yourself, and others too if you have a family, but again, it's fine to eat what you feel like and whatever is easiest at this stage. There were days where I had planned to cook something, only to feel unable to do so when it came to making the effort. That's completely okay, let yourself off the hook, and if you end up having more takeaways, cake or chocolate than usual, don't worry about it. In fact, take any small enjoyment where you can get it.

However, in time you will find it helpful, both physically and mentally, to get into a healthy, balanced eating routine because you will honestly feel better for doing so. The stress of grief and trauma can increase inflammation, affect your immune system, compromise your digestion and deplete your energy levels amongst other things, so the better your diet is, the stronger you will be physically. That, in turn, will have an effect on your emotional wellbeing.

There will be times, especially in early grief, when you will naturally retreat into denial in order to take a necessary break from the pain and reality of what has happened to you. This is normal. However, if we don't eventually fully process an emotional experience or trauma, or we try to suppress it, our body may store it for us, expressing it at a later date through physical pain, illness or disease.

Weight Loss or Weight Gain

Weight loss is common when you're in shock and unable to eat very much. Weight gain may come about if you begin to use food as a way to comfort yourself. You may even find you experience both at different stages of the grieving process. Be gentle on yourself. All being well, you will, given time, come back to a natural balance. If not, and either become problematic, please seek support from an appropriate professional.

Dehydration in Grief

Under a microscope, tears of grief are shown to have a different chemical make-up from other kinds of tears. It's thought that emotional tears contain stress hormones, which the body releases in the process of crying. Another theory is that crying triggers the body to release endorphins in order to make us feel better. It's certainly sometimes possible to feel better after a good cry but, during grief, it's equally possible it may not bring about much relief. That said, I believe it's still vital to cry whenever you feel the need to. Tears are part of healing. Never bottle them up. I cried, and still cry, a lot. It's thought that you can potentially become dehydrated from crying during intense grief. As it's known that dehydration can contribute to stress, anxiety and depression, it seems there may be multiple reasons why it's probably a very good idea to make sure you drink plenty of water during the grieving process.

Ideas for When You Have Little Appetite or Energy

If you find going to the supermarket a challenge, as I did, either swap to online shopping or, when someone asks you what they can do to help, ask them if they could shop for you. They may feel glad that they can do something practical for you.

The simplest idea for a relatively healthy breakfast is plain full fat yogurt with some fruit, nuts, seeds and a drizzle of honey. This requires little effort, it's pretty healthy and is easy on a stressed digestive system. It will also keep your blood sugar balanced.

For lunch, omelettes with any leftover vegetables are quick

and simple as well as nutritious, especially if you can manage to get together a salad on the side too. You may not feel up to making a soup initially, so a good quality one from the supermarket will do and may be a useful choice if you have little appetite. Try not to depend too much on sandwiches as the bread may be taxing on a delicate digestive system and may also further sap your precious energy.

I found one of the easiest evening meals for me to make and enjoy was roasted vegetables with grilled halloumi, lime and chilli. I found the repetitive chopping of peppers, aubergine, onions, sweet potatoes, and so on, quite soothing. Chicken or fish can replace the halloumi. Whatever you make in the early days, simple is best, and getting anything on the table can frankly be viewed as an achievement at this stage. It's not the end of the world to have more ready meals or takeaways whilst in the initial state of emergency. However, the danger is you remain in this habit so it's important to try to stay mindful that this way of eating is just short term.

The idea of being able to follow a recipe in the first few months seemed out of the question to me. I simply didn't have the energy or the brain capacity. In time, though, I did go back to making more complex meals and eating well again which felt like considerable progress, as well as a positive attempt to help myself feel as well as was possible under the circumstances.

Supplements

In view of the effects of grief and stress on our immune, nervous and digestive systems, a good quality multivitamin and mineral supplement can be viewed as valuable, if not essential back-up. This is especially true if you're either not eating very well or not eating enough. As stress affects the health of the gut microbiome, which is important for all aspects of health, it can be helpful to take a probiotic at this time too. Yogurt, kefir and other fermented foods are good for the microbiome if you have them regularly. As a nutritional therapist, I knew of various effective supplements for aiding sleep and for calming my nervous system and therefore anxiety. Eventually, and thankfully, these helped ease my physical symptoms.

I know it can be common for GPs to offer antidepressants to the bereaved, but if you prefer a drug-free approach, there are supplements that can help with mild to moderate depression and that have been shown in studies to be as effective as antidepressants but without the side effects. They can work rapidly, unlike antidepressants, and you don't need to be weaned off them. They won't deaden the pain, just lighten it, and you won't feel like a zombie. Studies have shown that mood-boosting serotonin can be depleted during bereavement and, as serotonin is manufactured in the gut, this is another reason why a probiotic might be helpful.

As nutritional therapists don't use a 'one size fits all' approach, I can't suggest specific protocols as people's circumstances are different and some supplements may be contraindicated with certain medication. Seeking the advice of a BANT-registered nutritional therapist for personalised advice on diet and supplements is a really good way to support yourself during the grieving process, particularly if you're struggling with anxiety, low mood, sleep, fatigue, digestive symptoms and so on. Being proactive and looking after yourself can give you back some control at a time when you feel like you have none.

See Appendix for details on how to find a registered nutritional therapist.

(Always consult your GP if you are unable to cope or suffer physical symptoms you are concerned about.)

Movement

There is now a lot of evidence to suggest that walking and being in nature help with grief, as well as anxiety and emotional wellbeing generally. Walking has benefited me considerably and I would put it very high on my list of things that have helped the most. Exercise is useful for expending the body's stress hormones, adrenaline and cortisol, which we know, if excessive, can be problematic during and after a trauma. Exercise also increases the levels of endorphins, the body's natural painkillers and mood boosters. Although I love walking, others might prefer running, cycling or going to the gym. Choose any form of activity that makes you feel (relatively) good. Now is not the time to do any form of exercise you don't really enjoy or that feels like too much of an effort. For me, in addition to walking, online 'yoga for grief' has been a life-saver. The simple breathing and stretching exercises have been invaluable for calming my anxiety and raising my mood from rock bottom. I can't recommend it highly enough. Because yoga combines movement with breathing, it can lead to a positive physiological and emotional response, calming an over-triggered nervous system and promoting relaxation, which has been shown to help with symptoms of PTSD.

See Appendix for 'yoga for grief' link.

Sleep

Not being able to sleep when you're grieving and/or traumatised can feel like additional torture. You can go to dark places at 3 a.m., or find you get unpleasant adrenaline rushes when you wake suddenly. You may be extremely sleep-deprived for the first few weeks but once the shock recedes somewhat and your nervous system calms, this should hopefully improve, albeit gradually. Supplements or herbs (on the recommendation of a qualified practitioner) can certainly help here and you could also try a sleep meditation. One of the simplest techniques I found was to count slowly back from 100 (I also visualised the number). You could also try the 4-7-8 technique (breathe in for a count of 4, hold for 7 and breathe out slowly through the mouth for 8), which will effectively calm your nervous system if you're feeling anxious.

Chapter 2

Counselling and Alternative Therapies for Bereavement

Very early on I decided I wanted bereavement counselling. Grief was not something I had much personal experience of. I had certainly not had a significant loss before and here I was starting with the biggest one of all. I knew I was very traumatised and, although I was using the tools I had to work on the physical manifestations of shock and trauma, there was the colossal emotional fallout from a sudden, out-of-order death to deal with.

That we were grieving together as a family seemed positive and speaking to friends helped enormously. I felt well supported, but I thought I needed experienced professional help in addition to this. I needed someone to guide me, someone who knew more than I did about what I was going through, and what was to come.

When looking for a therapist or counsellor be mindful of any who talk in terms of 'recovery', grief being a problem to be solved, or who adhere strictly to the concept of the linear Five Stages of Grief. Ask if they have substantial experience of your kind of grief, for example child loss, and of trauma, if applicable. Although it can be difficult in early grief, do try to consider what it is you want out of therapy or counselling. In hindsight, I didn't really do this and soon realised that sitting and stewing in my pain with a stranger wasn't for me and that (fortunately) I already had plenty of people to talk to in pretty much the same way I was doing with the counsellor. Other people may not feel they can talk to those around them and need their grief to be 'witnessed', so a therapist or counsellor may be helpful. Again, grief is so different for everyone. As a coach, I personally needed a more interactive, guided approach. I also wanted someone I felt truly 'got' my experience of losing a child – a big ask.

Therapy, of any kind, must serve *you*. There needs to be rapport and trust. If this isn't there then don't be afraid to move on and look at other therapists/therapies that might be more appropriate for you, conventional or otherwise. Just make sure you always check their training and experience. Read their reviews if they have them. All therapists and practitioners are going to be influenced by their own set of beliefs, often shaped by their own experiences, and this will inevitably inform how they work. This may or may not align with your own values and beliefs.

In the first part of this book, I described my experiences with both a bereavement counsellor and then a trauma therapist. Perhaps they weren't the best fit for me or perhaps my expectations were too high. I have met bereaved mothers who have been helped considerably by the right therapist or counsellor, and my daughter found bereavement counselling invaluable in helping her deal with the loss of her brother and the impact upon our family. But my stepdaughter didn't return a second time to a therapist she felt made no attempt at building rapport. She was met with a blank stare and silence when she asked if the therapist had ever experienced bereavement herself. I have also met many grieving mothers who haven't found therapy/counselling beneficial, and worse, some who actually had quite damaging experiences that made them feel more wretched than they already did. This is unacceptable when someone is reaching out for professional support in all good faith whilst experiencing the worst time of their life.

To me, this underlines a need for both a more sensitive and more specific approach for bereaved parents and their families and has led me to see the potential of offering my own form of grief support, where I can use my coaching experience (and nutritional therapy) to work holistically, as well as empathetically. I can draw on my own personal experience as a bereaved mother to offer gentle, compassionate guidance through the process I understand only too well. After all, in the end, only another bereaved parent can really know what this actually feels like.

Even as I rocked on my knees, howling, I detected soft breathing behind the roaring. I leaned in, listened. It was the murmuring of ten million mothers, backward and forward in time and right now, who had lost their children. They were lifting me, holding me. They had woven a net of their broken hearts and they were keeping me safe there. I realised that one day I would take my rightful place as a link in this web and I would hold my sister-mothers when their children died. For now, my only task was to grieve and be cradled in their love.

Mirabai Starr, *Caravan of No Despair*

Grief, Trauma and Mental Health

It's possible for grief and trauma to trigger mental health issues you didn't previously have. It's also possible for grief and trauma to trigger past issues you thought you'd worked through and left behind, such as anxiety or depression or even self-harming, addiction or eating disorders. (The latter issues, it goes without saying, will need specialist support.) Grief in itself isn't a mental health issue, but post-traumatic stress disorder (PTSD) is. However, PTSD is a mental health issue that's caused by something very specific, namely a traumatic event. Therefore, it's unfortunately quite common when there has been a sudden death and/or child loss. Sometimes, given time, PTSD symptoms may dissipate naturally, but sometimes they won't, in which case you will need to find appropriate and effective support and the nature of that support can vary from person to person.

Suicidal ideation is not unusual if your child has died and I feel it's important to take some of the stigma away if you feel/have felt like this. Although other books don't seem to broach this difficult subject, I've come to realise that it's relatively common to feel suicidal in maternal bereavement and so there really should be no shame around this subject. It is, after all, the very worst thing that can happen to any mother (or indeed father) and the agony of that loss is beyond words. But please remember it's highly likely that even if you feel suicidal on more than one occasion, you can eventually move beyond these feelings.

There may be days when you feel so low that you can't get out of bed and that you simply can't go on. This is hardly surprising when you've experienced such a terrible, life-shattering trauma. However, if you find that you don't have periods of time when you feel a bit better for a while, that you can't make the effort to shower or eat, that you're isolating yourself and fixating solely on not being here and on ways to take your life, then please seek support. (See Appendix.)

I have written that several times I felt my pain was just too great for me to bear, so I have complete understanding and compassion for you if you feel like that. Traumatic loss can take us to an alien place and we can feel so very far from the person we once were. Hold on to the belief that the pain can eventually ease and you won't always be without hope. I found writing about my feelings, vocalising my thoughts to those close to me, together with many of the suggestions I outline in this book, have helped me to step back from the precipice.

And whilst traditional bereavement counselling and trauma therapy didn't work out for me, I have found many other ways to support myself, both with a practitioner and on my own. There are so many different ways of supporting yourself through grief besides conventional therapy and counselling options. If, however, you have serious concerns about your physical or mental health, or you feel you are in danger of hurting yourself or others, you should always contact your GP.

Some of the therapies in the next section do not rely on the retelling of your story, but rather the physical implications in the present moment. This is perhaps one of the key differences between treating trauma and grief – with the latter, the importance of the telling and retelling of the bereavement story is considered key to moving through grief. However, when talk therapy won't on its own shift complicated grief or trauma, it is worth looking at physiological approaches such as body-based therapies and the creative arts.

Our bodies carry our experiences of traumatic events. *The Body Keeps the Score* by Bessel Van Der Kolk is highly recommended if you want to learn more about how trauma affects us both physically and mentally. Van Der Kolk says that the essence of trauma is that it is overwhelming, unbelievable and unbearable and that it robs you of the feeling that you are in charge of yourself. He also says, 'As long as the trauma is not resolved, the stress hormones that the body secretes to protect itself keep circulating...and the emotional responses keep getting replayed.' Therefore, talking therapies alone may have limited efficacy in cases of PTSD due to its physical as well as emotional/mental expression. In fact, Van Der Kolk notes a very interesting disparity between the experience of 9/11 trauma survivors and what worked best for them – namely acupuncture, massage, yoga and EMDR – and the recommendations of traditional talk therapies made by the experts.

When we are traumatised, the neural pathways in our brain cause us to perceive danger when there isn't any and this fear can keep us stuck. The more ingrained these neural pathways become, the more we are likely to repeat our reaction to a perceived threat. Repetitive thoughts make the grooves deeper, contributing to our suffering, as can repeatedly telling your story. It's a fine balance because we do initially need to tell our story many times, whether to friends or a counsellor/therapist. However, in the long term, this may not be entirely helpful if we want to heal and create new neural pathways.

Being in survival mode is meant to be a temporary phase that can help to save your life. It's not meant to be how you live once the immediate danger has passed. Unfortunately, sometimes when we endure experiences that wound us so deeply, survival systems remain active. These systems shift us onto a different, unfamiliar path, one we wouldn't be on if we hadn't been so disruptively traumatised.

The stress hormones of traumatised people can rise very rapidly and then take much longer to return to baseline. Consistently elevated stress hormones have many potential health implications, as outlined in the previous chapter, including memory issues, fatigue, difficulty sleeping, as well as very serious conditions such as cancer and heart disease. One of the best starting points for calming an over-triggered nervous system is nutritional therapy. From both personal and professional experience, I have seen that it's often easier to start working at a physical level before going on to the emotional issues.

Signs of trauma:

- **Psychological** – Reliving the trauma through a distressing recall of the event, flashbacks, and nightmares. Constantly thinking about the traumatic event. Being easily irritated and angered. Emotional numbness. Detachment. Disorientation. Feeling unreal. Overwhelm. Fear.
- **Physical** – Increased arousal and anxiety leading to disrupted sleep, inability to concentrate, feeling of being on high alert. Nausea, sweating, trembling, pain.

- **Social** – Avoiding places and people that might remind you of the trauma (though even ones that don't directly do so can still provoke anxiety). Becoming isolated and withdrawn. Giving up activities you once enjoyed. Loss of purpose.

Other Therapies

The following modalities favour a holistic approach to healing the body, mind and spirit. All can potentially help with processing grief and trauma but it's crucial to find what's right for you as an individual – and also a very good and experienced practitioner. And, of course, it goes without saying that just because something helped me, it doesn't necessarily mean it will help you in the same way.

Information about where to find practitioners can be found in the Appendix.

Reiki

Whilst Reiki is considered an 'alternative therapy', there are actually numerous studies to be found citing it as a potentially effective treatment for anxiety and depression. Reiki definitely helped me in the early stages of grief. I cried through most of the sessions but felt they calmed my anxiety and helped me sleep better and I just felt a little more able to cope after a session. Reiki practitioners typically place their hands on or above areas of the body that they believe need a boost and will assist in the body's natural healing processes. Reiki is thought to promote emotional, mental and spiritual wellbeing and to induce deep relaxation, relieve emotional stress and improve overall wellbeing. This form of 'energy healing' might not be for everyone but I have included it here because I personally found it beneficial.

EMDR

Eye Movement Desensitisation and Reprocessing (EMDR) is a form of psychotherapy which is gaining credibility for treating PTSD. When I first found out about EMDR I was so hopeful that this could be a way of helping me with the trauma I experienced, the flashbacks and ongoing anxiety it had left me with. Unfortunately, I found it made me more anxious; I really don't know why this was the case. However, this hasn't stopped me believing that it can, for some people, be an effective way of addressing trauma and I may try it again with a different therapist at a later date if I feel I still need help with processing my trauma. The fact that it doesn't rely on talk or medication may make it particularly appropriate for some. This is also one form of 'alternative' help which may be available on the NHS.

EFT

EFT stands for Emotional Freedom Technique and is sometimes called 'Psychological Acupressure' or tapping. It's a scientifically proven technique that works to rewire the brain by sending calming signals to the amygdala, the stress centre of the brain, allowing both the body and brain to release emotional blockages. These techniques are being accepted increasingly in medical and psychiatric circles as well as in the range of psychotherapies and healing disciplines. EFT is considered beneficial for trauma, anxiety and depression. The treatment involves the use of fingertips to tap on the end points of energy meridians that are situated just beneath the surface of the skin whilst focusing on an emotional trigger in order to release it.

Havening

Havening comes from the word 'haven', meaning a safe space. This is another technique to consider if you're suffering from PTSD. I was shown how to do this by my coaching mentor, and I found it had a definite calming effect. It's a touch therapy that can boost serotonin and reduce anxiety. There are plenty of YouTube videos showing the techniques (including some with Paul McKenna, who is an advocate for Havening) but again, it's a case of deciding whether it's going to be right for you and if it's worth a try. The way I was shown how to use it was with downward strokes from shoulders to elbows repeating certain phrases such as: 'I am here, I am safe, this is now' whenever you find yourself reliving a traumatic event. As the mind doesn't know the difference between a thought and something that's actually happening, in some ways when we remember the trauma, we really are reliving it. Using words in the present tense together with the physical strokes can help bring us into the now.

According to havening.org:

The Havening Techniques are a healing modality that is designed to help individuals overcome problems that are the consequence of traumatic encoding...The Havening Techniques can be used within a psychotherapeutic setting with professional mental health care clinicians who have been fully trained and certified in The Havening Techniques. In addition, The Havening Techniques can be used by non-licensed practitioners as a protocol for coaching sessions or as a tool in allied health care practice by individuals who have been fully trained and certified in The Havening Techniques. The Havening Techniques can also be used as a self-help technique and shared with family members and friends.

Aromatherapy, Acupuncture, Reflexology

These are all alternative therapies that can calm the nervous system and potentially help you release some of the physical symptoms you may have, as well as the inevitable emotional build-up. They all come under the umbrella of self-care, and aromatherapy and reflexology treatments (though perhaps not acupuncture) are enjoyable experiences, and this is undoubtedly welcome during grief. As previously mentioned, traumatised survivors of 9/11 cited acupuncture as one of the therapies that helped them the most.

Look for individual practitioners in your area, check their reviews and ask if they have any experience of working with bereaved clients or PTSD, if that's relevant to you. All 'touch therapies' have the potential to trigger an emotional response so a practitioner who is experienced and trauma-informed could be vital.

Chapter 3

Ways to Heal

You are not the darkness you endured.
You are the light that refused to surrender.
John Mark Green

Healing is about living despite the pain of loss. The author Tom Zuba (who lost two children and his wife) says that when it comes to grief, healing isn't a destination but rather an ongoing process. He says, 'Healing has become my way of being in the world.' He also says it's possible for the connection with our loved ones to grow stronger the more we heal. I would agree with this.

I don't think we necessarily fully comprehend the enormity of our loss and trauma in the very early weeks because it would just be too much. We might also find early on that we experience a kind of action paralysis. It may therefore be easier, if you can possibly manage it, to initially try some of the suggestions from Chapter 2 that resonate with you, as they involve the guidance of a practitioner. Some, though not all, of the ideas in this chapter may be more appropriate when you are beyond those first few weeks and are feeling up to being a little more proactive. As always, though, it's different for everyone.

Also, it's probably important to say in a chapter titled 'Ways to Heal' that just simply being kind to yourself is vital to your healing. It may be a natural response to feel you failed in some way to protect your child or loved one from dying – but that doesn't make it true. When we're hurting, we need to take care of ourselves first and foremost as we recover from such a critical wound. We can't do much positive thinking in the initial stages of the nightmare or whilst we are trying to fathom the enormity of what just happened. For a while, we may stop trusting our intuition. Why wouldn't we? We know now that really terrible things do happen. Maybe we didn't see it coming, and as a result, the rug was well and truly pulled out from under us, leaving us disorientated and confused. So, it may take a little time for us to trust ourselves again, or indeed to believe that the world can be a good place. That's fine, but try to find little ways that help you to work through what's happened. I hope some of the ideas below work for you.

Journaling

Writing can be an excellent way to process what has happened and there are studies that show it's beneficial for anxiety, depression and heart health. I recommend that you write without a filter, just for yourself, so that you're not hindered by what people might think. Write from you and for you. When you write freely, the writing can move in a certain way on its own, so try to let it be organic as this will be the most beneficial to you in terms of emotional pain relief. They say writing about trauma gives you back your voice. I found it provided some much-needed peace in the midst of intense heartache. You may choose to write about very difficult moments, as I did, but you don't have to relive them. To stop the loop in my brain I told myself as I wrote about finding Harry dead: 'I'm not finding Harry today, Harry isn't dying today. He is safe where he is and I'm safely sitting at my desk. That was then, this is now.' We didn't have control when our loved one died but we do now, and having some sort of control through writing about my experiences has been invaluable to me. Witnessing your own story by getting everything you're feeling down on paper can create a safe distance from what happened. It can be incredibly healing and has without doubt been one of the best forms of therapy for me.

In addition to journaling, you may like to try the following.

Write to your child or the person you lost, telling them anything you feel you need to say and asking them any questions you'd like answered by them. Then reply, as them, back to you. I did this as part of a Helping Parents Heal group of bereaved parents and it was incredible how the words from our children just flowed from the pen, more so than when we wrote to them! It was an emotional exercise but very cathartic and we all felt very close to our child as we did this.

Bibliotherapy

The definition of bibliotherapy: 'the reading of specific texts with the purpose of healing'.

This is also right up there as one of the activities that kept me going. Reading isn't necessarily thought of as 'healing' or 'therapy' but it was, and still is, for me. Initially, it helped me to understand what grief is, how other people experience it and what happens after death. All of which felt imperative early on. Though I've always been a big reader, I have never read so many books in such a short space of time. I do urge you to see if it's a useful way to navigate your loss. Reading about other bereaved mothers who survived the death of their child, and also about life after death, has given me hope that I can continue to live, despite what has happened to me. I must add that, in addition, having a novel on the go was, and is, so helpful in providing much-needed distraction and space away from the pain, particularly at that dangerous flash-point before you go to sleep.

In the Appendix, you will find my recommended books on grief. I've learnt something from most of the books I've read during bereavement, but I have narrowed my list down to the ones I feel helped me the most. It's therefore a very personal list but my hope is, if these books helped me, they might help others too. There is a separate book list in the Appendix for those who are interested in exploring the subject of life after death.

Meditation and Visualisation

Meditation and mindfulness are really quite mainstream now and it's well known that they can help with the stress of our modern-day lives, but are they useful when we're grieving? Research shows that meditation measurably reduces pain and anxiety, boosts the immune system and increases concentration, focus and compassion – so apparently, yes. In addition, it helps us live in the present moment so can give us a break if we find we are endlessly ruminating on what happened in the past or fixated on feelings of hopelessness when we consider the future. It is even thought to provide the nervous system with a rest that is five times deeper than sleep, so it's worth trying if insomnia is an issue. Meditation can also help us manage other physical symptoms of grief, such as muscle tension, headaches, and unpleasant feelings in the chest or stomach. Using the breath in meditation will help soothe the nervous system and promote a better sense of wellbeing. I like both the Calm and Headspace apps, but personally, I have found it more helpful to use guided meditations and visualisations during grief. Focusing on specific instructions can be more appropriate at such a challenging time when your mind understandably wanders to upsetting thoughts or images.

During a meditation, some people report feeling more connected with a higher power and feeling their vibrational energy level rise. Some believe your frequency can begin to vibrate on a different level and that you may feel a shift in your feelings, thoughts, and/or in the physical body. Because I've been going in a more spiritual direction, I've used the guided meditations that I've found via Hay House, Gabrielle Bernstein and Claire Broad.

Sound for Healing

The concept of sound baths originated in Tibet around 2000 years ago. They have nothing to do with water – a sound bath is a relaxation technique and meditative experience where you 'bathe' in the sound waves produced by the human voice or instruments such as chimes, gongs, drums and singing bowls. You don't have to do anything, just relax and let the sounds wash over you. Although there are actual places you can go for a sound bath, you can listen to crystal 'singing' bowls on YouTube (I like the 11-minute 'Chakra Tune Up' from Temple Sounds). There is a different bowl, and therefore sound, for each chakra and so you can visualise the colour for each one and may even feel something physically in each area of the body where the chakra is centred. Sound baths can provide a 'reset' when you're feeling overwhelmed and, for me personally, they also offer the added dimension of being something I feel Harry, as a musician, would be interested in and therefore they provide me with an additional source of connection.

This is also true for the so-called Hz frequencies or Solfeggio frequencies which refer to tones of sound that are purported to promote the health of the mind, body and spirit. The frequencies balance and aid healing by the effect the sounds have on the conscious and unconscious mind. The frequencies are thought to date back to various ancient traditions and, more recently, science has shown that they can impact our DNA. Our cells are responsive to frequency and vibration, so the potential for these frequencies to be used as a component in healing our grief or trauma is worth considering. At the very least, they are very relaxing to listen to. You can find Hz frequencies or Solfeggio frequencies on YouTube.

Essential Oils

Essential oils have been important throughout my grief and PTSD, helping to restore a little of my mental, emotional and energetic wellbeing. Apparently, the smell from certain essential oils directly impacts the limbic system, the region of the brain that activates our fight-or-flight response, potentially helping with the release of emotional trauma. As we know, when people have been traumatised, this is the part of the brain that is the most affected.

I mainly use doTerra oils but Neals Yard and Tisserand are good too. I use Lavender and Rose for anxiety and restful sleep. I also like Rose Geranium and Orange as they feel uplifting and give me a little boost, but the ones I've used the most are two doTerra blends. One is called Reassuring blend for anxiety, and the other is called Console blend, which is indicated for grief. I sometimes put them in the diffuser but, more often than not, I rub them together in the palm of my hands and inhale. When I do this, I feel a noticeable difference and a subtle shift in how I'm feeling; they definitely take the edge off the emotional pain or any anxiety and can help a bout of crying to taper off. There is a safety issue with some essential oils so please seek advice, if necessary, from a qualified aromatherapist. My understanding is that only doTerra oils can be used directly on the skin.

Crystals

Crystals may not take away the pain of grief and their benefits have not been proven by science but, in my experience, they can soothe the soul a little. I like the idea that different crystals have different properties. I do notice a subtle energy or vibration when holding them, though I can't say I feel noticeably better when I do so (in contrast to when I use essential oils). Holding crystals or placing them on your body is thought to promote physical, emotional and spiritual healing by positively interacting with your body's energy field. I think when you are suffering from trauma and grief, simply holding something solid and beautiful can be a comfort in itself. If they also give off some beneficial vibration, then so much the better. I have found myself acquiring more and more of them and they give me pleasure – and that alone is not to be undervalued when you're experiencing the worst time of your life.

Crystals that are thought to be particularly beneficial for grief include Black Obsidian, Lepidolite, Apache Tear, Amethyst, Rose Quartz and Smoky Quartz.

Chapter 4

Building Resilience and Continuing Bonds

I'll soak every moment in,
try as hard as I can to spread every ounce of love,
try as I can to live for a reason, so that on that day,
I'll run and tell you everything I was able to do, not for me.
But because of you.
Every day is one day closer to you.
Lexi Behrndt

Nature

Being outside in the fresh air, and walking where there were trees and grass, made a difference to me right from the start. Living in London, parks and my back garden had to suffice, but just reminding myself of the vastness of the sky seemed important when my world had shrunk, and if the sun was out and had a little warmth to it, I could even feel a fleeting appreciation for life. Of course, observing the seasons reminds us that death is a part of the cycle of life (a particularly difficult concept if you've lost your child which is not the natural order of things) but also that there is hope with the spring.

Walking in nature is known to help with our mental wellbeing. Studies show that exposure to nature is equal to physical exercise in its health gains. I found just sitting in my garden reading, with my feet on the grass grounding me, made me feel more relaxed and helped my mood. The latter was probably also because I was getting some vitamin D, which is important for depression and anxiety amongst so many other things. (It's a good idea to ask your GP to test your vitamin D levels and take a supplement if necessary. The majority of clients I see are deficient in this very important vitamin.)

Quite early on, I felt the need to plant flowers in pots and in the garden, including roses for Harry. Getting your hands in the soil, helping things to grow, tending to them and watching them bloom is definitely therapeutic, so I would highly recommend gardening, too.

Travel

Going to the seaside, whether to the south coast of England or to northern France, was very restorative during our first summer of loss and this remains an important aspect of my healing. It certainly played an integral part in helping me survive the first few months. The distraction of being somewhere other than home, where no one knew what had happened to us, as well as the relaxing negative ions from the sea, helped ease some of the pain. If you live in a city, the healing benefits of breathing fresh air for a change also help. Trips away not only gave me something to look forward to but seemed to save me from what seemed like unending misery.

That said, I do know some bereaved parents who didn't feel ready to leave the safety of home, particularly during the first year, so it's a very individual choice. Although it was helpful for us, we kept things simple and didn't travel too far. I wouldn't have felt up to airports or going to a specific holiday destination where we had gone to as a 'complete' family.

Social Media

Social media, as we all know, can be toxic. It can also be enormously helpful if you're following the right people or in the right groups. Prior to Harry's death, I mainly followed people or pages promoting a healthy lifestyle and a positive attitude to life, which was fine at the time. However, once I was plunged into my unasked-for new world, some of this no longer resonated and instead had the potential to make me feel worse than I already did. I would literally shout at the screen as I saw all these chirpy posts from people, including well-known spiritual or motivational 'gurus', who I felt demonstrated no understanding of what it was to suffer something as truly terrible as I had. Unfortunately, I can no longer simply 'choose happiness' as they advocate. The relentless quest to be happy, prevalent in certain areas of social media with its emphasis on only 'good' emotions and its disregard of the 'bad' ones, is clearly problematic for those experiencing traumatic grief. Valid human emotions getting dismissed as 'negative' is known as 'toxic positivity'.

So, I started to follow new people and join groups that were more relevant to my current situation. In essence, my social media feed became all about grief. I soon learned that it's not necessarily a good idea to replace the annoyingly positive people with those who are visibly grieving, particularly people whose grief remains raw many years down the line. For some people, the pain never eases and I eventually found it unhelpful to read that the pain of losing a child doesn't ever change. For me, it's not beneficial to have that message constantly in my face, particularly during early grief when you may feel inclined to believe anything you read if it's written by someone who has walked in your shoes. We simply can't predict the future of our own personal grief journey but I find it helps me to hope that I won't remain stuck or completely broken and so I've made the decision to try to heal. Tom Zuba says if you don't believe you can heal, then you won't...

I also started following people and pages that promote a spiritual message that life isn't over when you die and that our loved ones are still around us. This may not be for everyone, but for me it has helped enormously. However, if you do the same, be careful of 'spiritual bypassers'. A spiritual bypass or spiritual bypassing (a term coined by John Welwood, a Buddhist teacher and psychotherapist) is a 'tendency to use spiritual ideas and practices to sidestep or avoid facing unresolved emotional issues, psychological wounds, and unfinished developmental tasks'. Also, most definitely avoid all practitioners/therapists who try to minimise your experience in any way. A skilled practitioner (or motivational speaker) should never suggest you either deny or 'rise above' your grief through some kind of spiritual practice.

Generally speaking, my advice is to cull everything on social media that is no longer in tune with your new existence and follow people and pages that resonate in the present moment. You may be drawn to closed Facebook groups for the bereaved, as I was, but if you find they are pulling you down, you may want to look for more balanced alternatives. As a bereaved person, you're already in pain – but you don't need to actively feed that pain, so look for those groups that acknowledge the reality of a tragic bereavement but that also demonstrate a hope that grief can at least soften, that your bond continues and, if appropriate to you, a belief that all life continues, just in a different form.

It's such a fine line between acknowledging the terrible loss and pain that you're in and having hope that, whilst you will never ever get over what's happened, you *can* have a life, taking your loved one with you as you go forward. In my view, any page or group that you're a part of, or book you read, or therapist or support group, needs to demonstrate an understanding that this is the healthiest way forward. They are all, in the end, just 'tools' to serve you in navigating the choppy waters of grief. Don't let anything prevent you from moving forward or fail to acknowledge that, as you do go forward, your loved one is still very much a part of you.

Creativity

Pain needs expression and creativity can be an outlet. Creative expression can bring us out of our head and into our heart and help us to access the deeper layers of ourselves. You probably won't feel like doing any of the suggestions below during the early months (I certainly didn't) but eventually, further down the line, you may feel ready to give one or two a try.

At my Compassionate Friends group, several of the women have found pottery to be really therapeutic. You could also consider painting, knitting, mosaics, all of which you can lose yourself in for a few hours and feel a sense of accomplishment about what you produce.

Singing also provides many benefits, including lowering stress levels and aiding sleep, so joining a choir might be an option. Dance/movement can have therapeutic potential too, not focusing on technique or performance but instead the creative, expressive process. Trauma can leave us feeling anxious and hyper-alert and dance brings us into our bodies, helping to ground us, to develop breath support and to feel more in control, as well as being another way of expressing ourselves.

At around six months, I found making framed collages very therapeutic. I used photos of my son, flowers I had pressed from the funeral bouquet and sentences printed off from poems that resonated with me. I found I really enjoyed the creativity of the activity. This would also come under Continuing Bonds (below).

For many years I created a vision board, but after Harry died, the one I'd done most recently made no sense to me any more and I took it down. At around nine months, I created another one, a very different one. It has photos of Harry when he was young, along with poems and affirmations that feel appropriate to me at this stage. Needless to say, these are gentle and realistic but also hopeful. As I have my vision board on my desk, I look at it daily and change it up as I move along in this journey.

Continuing Bonds

As long as you are alive, so, too, is your relationship with your child alive...Instead of severing our bond, to mourn means to maintain a continuing relationship and to integrate our loved one into our life in a new way.

Nisha Zenoff, *The Unspeakable Loss*

I am relieved that 'letting go', 'finding closure' or 'getting over' your loss is no longer an expectation in the way that it once was. Bear this in mind if anyone (friend, acquaintance or therapist) tells you otherwise. I think 'moving forward' is healthy but 'moving on' probably isn't. To me, moving on suggests we should leave our loved one behind and try not to think or talk about them. 'Moving forward' suggests taking them with us into the future, as does 'move with'.

I won't ever move on, let go, find closure or get over the loss of my son. I feel connected to him still and I expect to continue to feel that way forever. Although I feel part of me died when he died, I also strongly feel part of him lives on with the new me. The connection often seems tangible. Harry informs who I now am and how I live the rest of my life – and I like that.

Apparently, our children literally live on in us. I was gladdened to discover that some of our children's cells continue to live in us after they are born, particularly those from male foetuses. Mothers and foetuses exchange DNA and cells, and research has shown that some of these cells live in our blood and bones for decades. It's called foetal microchimerism. As a bereaved mother, I find it incredibly comforting to know that our children live on in us – literally.

Continuing bonds can help us process our grief in a very healing way that potentially reduces some of the aching. Research has found that remaining connected to our loved ones seems to facilitate the ability of the bereaved to cope with loss and the subsequent changes to their lives. It was observed that healthy grieving did not resolve by detaching from the deceased, but instead by creating a new relationship with them. I like the view that your relationship is never over, simply changed. This makes perfect sense to me. I'm still Harry's mum and I always will be. Continuing to think about him, to find ways to honour him, and even talk to him, feels right to me. I love remembering how wonderful he was, and I like talking about him. This is, for me at least, an important part of coming to terms with his physical absence.

Ways to Honour Your Loved One

There are some that bring a light so great to the world
that even after they have gone,
the light remains.
Unknown

There are many ways to honour the person you have lost. It's said that grief is the price we pay for love, and honouring them is a way of continuing your bond and expressing that love. Here are a few ways we, and Harry's friends, have chosen to honour him so far:

- A memorial bench in the local park.
- An inscribed slate plaque in our garden, where we also place flowers and light candles.
- Rose bushes planted in memory of Harry (we bought ours from The Compassionate Friends website).
- A memory book that everyone who knew him can write in. This is an incredibly precious record for us of how he touched the lives of everyone who knew him.
- Making collages (see 'Creativity' above).
- Even though we aren't religious, we like to go into

churches and light a candle for Harry, then sit and think of him.

- We buy and light candles for him regularly at home too and particularly, of course, for birthdays and anniversaries.
- Start a collection. Without really realising, I seem to have been collecting angel wings and angels made from various types of crystal. I have also started to look for heart-shaped pebbles on beaches and I place these by his plaque.
- Wear their clothes or jewellery. I wear a necklace of Harry's which I never take off. I also wear his sweatshirts and one of his coats. Lily sometimes wears his T-shirts to sleep in. On Christmas Day we all wear one of his shirts.
- Write a letter to them, a poem about them, or write the story of their life.
- We have over 80 songs as part of Harry's legacy, some of which are now on Spotify.
- Continue with an interest they enjoyed. Harry loved to take photographs using old camera film. I don't do that but I have found I've been taking more photos on my walks which I sometimes post on Instagram. I love the link photography has given us, because it's a new link, one that has only come about after Harry's passing.
- Most people who have had a devastating loss seem to find it helps them to give back in some way. We had a music night and a gym challenge in the first year, raising money for a music scholarship in Harry's name.
- On the first birthday after Harry's death, we dedicated a star to him and on the day shared the details with everyone who knew him.
- For his most recent birthday, I put together an e-book using Canva. I asked his friends to contribute memories and stories of Harry, as well as photos. This gave me a

'project' in those dreaded days leading up to a birthday. It was also really uplifting to hear stories that I hadn't heard before, some of which were very funny. Sharing this tribute to Harry on the day of his birthday helped dissipate some of the inevitable poignancy of his physical absence on such a significant date.

- Some bereaved families set up a website with photos and videos. This can be somewhere for family and friends to post any stories they have about him.

- Jack and Jessie (Harry's half-siblings) and some of Harry's friends have had tattoos done in his honour.

- At Christmas time, we gave some of Harry's shoes and a coat to a homeless charity and donated a trolley filled with his favourite food too.

- We keep a jar of Marmite (which has Harry's name on – a present in his Christmas stocking one year) permanently on the kitchen table, like a place setting. That way Harry is always with us when we sit down for a meal. This acts like evidence that Harry lived here, was part of our family and that he always will be.

I'm sure there are many more ideas besides these – do whatever feels like a good way to remember them and to keep them with you.

The 'Teaspoon Drawer' Moment

When I read the book *Resilient Grieving* by Lucy Hone (see Appendix for my book list), I was struck that the author, whilst acknowledging we have to grieve fully, says that sometimes we need to engage in some small activity to break a period where we literally can't move or we've been crying for ages. She calls it the 'cleaning-out-the-teaspoon-drawer moment' so that your brain switches from abject misery and persistent rumination to a purpose, albeit a trivial, mindless one. Sometimes we just need a break from it all and I found clearing out a wardrobe or a cupboard does make me feel better. It can provide a temporary distraction, breaking an emotional groove I have found myself stuck in.

Post-traumatic Growth

Pain and suffering can break and destroy us or they can crack us open and create growth, love, and strength. We often hear of post-traumatic stress but we forget about post-traumatic growth and how they often exist simultaneously.
Nell Rose Forman

Despite the anguish of living on without someone you love and the negative implications of post-traumatic stress disorder, there is also the possibility of cultivating post-traumatic growth. Both Lucy Hone and David Kessler mention this in their books (see book list in Appendix). Pain can have a purpose in shifting our perception of life and there are several ways you can grow after a tragedy. These include discovering a new purpose in life; helping others who have experienced a similar tragedy; becoming more compassionate; a deepening spirituality; discovering an inner strength you perhaps didn't know you had; and developing stronger relationships. Having experienced both post-traumatic stress disorder and post-traumatic growth, I feel that they are two sides of the same coin. And I know which one I prefer.

However, it's important not to feel any pressure to turn pain into purpose – to have to transform it into something meaningful. It can certainly help, but not if it bypasses the healing of your grief and trauma. There are times we have to allow the pain to just be. I find this to be a fine balance and one that I'm still working on.

Personal development, where we reframe our narratives and thoughts in a more positive way, is great for many aspects of our growth, but when grief and trauma are present, matters may be far more complex. Based on my own experience up to this point, I feel that the best path through grief is to fill your toolbox with ways to support yourself, look for purpose in life where you can, but combine this with allowing the pain to rise up when it wants to without suppression, granting it the expression it requires. Allowing yourself to fully experience the pain of your grief isn't a negative thing to be avoided; it's necessary for the ongoing process of healing.

Whilst you aim to find this balance, you may find that your reduced resilience and increased feeling of vulnerability put additional obstacles in your way. This has been my experience but, of course, it won't necessarily be true for everyone. However, it can be very disconcerting to find you seem to lack the resilience you might once have possessed. I have spoken in Part One about how very vulnerable and exposed I felt. This feeling has somewhat lessened as I try to work towards post-traumatic growth and re-establishing resilience, but for me, it can still take very little to set me back. I hope, in time, this will improve. Setting little goals for myself and focusing on small achievements helps. I'm also good at saying no to things I don't want to do.

One piece of advice I read many times, and very much agree with, is to avoid making any major decisions in the first year or so of grief. You may find you have flashes of impetuosity (I know I did) but major changes such as moving house, changing your job or getting divorced are best delayed until you're sure you once more have the strength and resilience to deal with any additional stress such a change might bring.

Developing Your Spiritual Life and Connection

Embrace your grief, for there your soul will grow.
Carl Jung

This has been an important aspect of helping me to survive my loss. It began, as I have already said, when I first saw Harry's body, like an empty chrysalis he'd left behind, and I felt, with great clarity, that he continued to exist 'somewhere else'. I fully realise this is an area that some people are sceptical about, usually citing the lack of scientific proof to support it. I also realise that not everyone who is bereaved feels as I do – there are those who had some type of faith prior to a tragic event but go on to lose it afterwards, and others who have a religious faith which may preclude some of the following. As always, these are my own personal views, formed by the experience of losing my child.

There have been studies that estimate a high percentage of bereaved people believe they have had one or more after-death communication (ADCs) within a year of bereavement and, according to Raymond Moody MD, PhD, 75% of bereaved parents believe they have had a communication from their child. This surprising prevalence of perceived after-death communication is rarely acknowledged. It seems very possible – at least to me – that the trauma and intensity of a significant loss can lead, in some cases, to a spiritual awakening that facilitates this communication.

Whilst I in no way seek to persuade anyone to believe what I've come to believe, I take solace from being in good company and the fact that there is quite a lot of ongoing research in this fascinating area. Gary E Schwartz, PhD, director of the University of Arizona's Laboratory for Advances in Consciousness and Health, a former assistant professor at Harvard and tenured professor at Yale, says: *'Speaking as a scientist, I am now 99.9 percent certain that life continues after bodily death.'* Retired lawyer Victor Zammit, PhD, is in agreement and states: 'The evidence collected would be accepted by the highest court in any civilized country.'

Carl Sagan, astronomer and astrophysicist, said: 'Science is not only compatible with spirituality; it is a profound source of spirituality.' And Albert Einstein said: 'Everyone who is seriously involved in the pursuit of science becomes convinced that some spirit is manifest in the laws of the universe, one that is vastly superior to that of man.'

Whether or not these eminent men are correct in their summations, it is, in the end, up to the individual to make up their own mind. If someone hasn't had a cataclysmic life-changing experience, it's probably difficult to understand how those of us that have can potentially become more open to the possibility that this life is not all there is.

Interestingly, those who believe in an afterlife apparently fare better in the grieving process than those who don't. I've read several studies where scholars have argued that belief in an afterlife may help individuals cope better with the death of a loved one. They conclude that afterlife beliefs can provide a sense of meaning during times of despair, fostering continued emotional attachments with the deceased. A study in the *BMJ* (*British Medical Journal*) concluded: 'People who profess stronger spiritual beliefs seem to resolve their grief more rapidly and completely after the death of a close person than do people with no spiritual beliefs.' I'm not sure my own experience bears out this last statement – I don't expect my grief to be 'resolved' and no part of my grieving process appears to be rapid – but I do feel this development in my spiritual life has helped me to survive the trauma of my child's physical death.

Without doubt, the passing of someone we love greatly can throw all we previously thought to be reality into question, and my world has certainly shifted beyond anything I could have imagined. This kind of shift can lead to seeking a way to connect with the person you have lost and, for some, mediums facilitate this link, offering confirmation that a loved one's spirit is still around them, as well as reassurance that they are fine. The majority of mediums, in my experience, are genuine and their work can potentially bring about a perceptible abatement of the pain of loss for many bereaved people. I acknowledge that bereaved people can be vulnerable but, although there will inevitably be some charlatans out there, I don't accept that all mediums are out to exploit us as a group. However, even though they have helped me, I realise consulting a medium won't be an appropriate way for everyone to support their grieving process.

Interestingly, though, research has shown that a positive experience with a medium is considerably more effective at easing the pain of bereavement than conventional psychological or counselling techniques. This was true in my case. People often turn to mediums because the spiritual element is missing in traditional bereavement counselling, so there is clearly a need here that is not being met.

I respect anyone who doesn't believe there is anything more after death, as I hope they respect my belief that there is. If, however, you decide to see a medium, make sure you choose carefully, do your research and ideally go by recommendation.

See the Appendix for the mediums that I've had sessions with, as well as a list of books on life after death. Please always make your own informed decisions.

Helping Parents Heal

Lastly in this section, I want to mention an organisation called Helping Parents Heal which was set up by some very inspirational bereaved parents in the USA and is dedicated to providing resources to aid in the healing process. They allow the open discussion of spiritual experiences and evidence for the afterlife, in a non-dogmatic way, and parents can safely share their experiences. They believe, as I do, that there are many factors that contribute to the healing process, acknowledging that 'in addition to support from family, friends and other bereaved parents, some find peace and a sense of purpose in learning more about the continuation of consciousness after physical death'.

If this is something that might be of interest to you, then you can sign up to their newsletter, watch their videos on YouTube or join their closed Facebook groups. The main American Facebook group is very large, but in Britain there is a branch called Helping Parents Heal UK which is much smaller and so, for me, preferable. Unlike a lot of Facebook groups for the bereaved, Helping Parents Heal, due to the underlying premise that our children are still with us, gets much less bogged down by overwhelming outpourings of pain which can sometimes be so hard to witness. Most branches, including the UK one, have regular Zoom meetings, often with guest speakers and mediums, and the sessions are usually very uplifting. There is also a sub-branch called Helping Siblings Heal UK run by the daughter of one of the members which is for young people who have an interest in a spiritual connection with their sibling. If your other children don't have this interest but are looking for a support group, then The Compassionate Friends also offer support and connection for siblings. (See Appendix.)

One of my motivations for writing this book was that there were so few I read that were written by bereaved parents in the UK. I'm very thankful for all the incredible books I read that are written by American authors who lost a child but sometimes I just longed to read about a British mum and see a few relatable British references, as well as an accessible resource list. The same goes for groups, which is why Helping Parents Heal UK and The Compassionate Friends UK may feel more accessible than their larger US counterparts. That said, all do an amazing job in supporting bereaved parents wherever they may live and I am thankful for discovering them all.

Chapter 5

Who Can Help You Heal

Family, friends and pets can all play a major part in your healing. We can't get through this alone, so we need a support network of some sort around us. Our family members are grieving with us, so we need people outside the family.

First, a word about siblings and grandparents. They can get a bit overlooked when they've lost a brother, sister or grandchild, as the focus is often on the parents who've lost a child (or partner if they had one).

Grandparents have the double issue of dealing with the loss of an adored grandchild whilst they themselves live on into old age. They also have to witness their own child in terrible distress, which they are unable to ease. They may lack support if many of their own elderly friends have already died, and the family tragedy may weaken their already declining physical state. Living a long life, whilst their grandchild didn't, can lead them to experience 'survivor's guilt'. However, they may come from a generation who don't always seek help and are sometimes stoical in the face of grief. There is a good section on The Compassionate Friends website for grandparents (see Appendix).

Young people who've lost a sibling often find their friends lack the emotional maturity to support them. Some friends may quickly stop mentioning the dead brother or sister of the bereaved young person, which can seem like a lack of care, but they may simply not know what to say. In addition, the sibling may not feel they can burden their grieving parents with their own pain. They may well feel that they've lost their parents as well as their sibling and that their parents are no longer able to support them as they once used to. They may struggle to see their parents so altered by grief. This can be frightening and destabilising to witness. It may also make them angry. Then there's the question: 'Do you have any brothers or sisters?' (Parents and grandparents have to deal with their own version of this now dreaded question.) Altogether it's a great deal for a young person to cope with, so some form of therapy or counselling may need to be offered to them.

My experience is of losing an adult child and having a remaining child who was 20 at the time of his death. The loss of an only child, or a much younger child, and having to cope with siblings who are also very young, brings a different set of challenges which I haven't experienced. I recommend The Compassionate Friends as a starting point for finding support for your particular circumstances.

The family unit will never be the same again and there's just no getting around this. The family dynamic has altered, and a sibling is likely to have changed their position in the family and in many cases become an only child. To lose a brother or sister at a tender age is a terrible thing to happen and it will undoubtedly shape them in a very significant way. But hopefully, siblings will one day have their own families with their own children and life will go on for them in a way that it can't for their parents. However, the prospect of seeing any remaining children lead fulfilling lives, not to mention providing grandchildren, can be a good reason to continue to live on for parents and can provide some hope of a future that contains a little joy.

Compassionate Friends offers various kinds of support for siblings, such as retreat weekends, Facebook groups and newsletters. There is also quite a lot of sibling grief support for young people available on social media, particularly Instagram.

Friends

The friend who can be silent with us in a moment of despair or confusion, who can stay with us in an hour of grief and bereavement,

who can tolerate not knowing, not curing, not healing and face
with us the reality of our powerlessness, that is a friend who cares.
Henri Nouwen

I couldn't have managed without my friends. They were a lifeline in early grief. They visited me when I couldn't go out, walked with me whatever the weather and sat outside cafes when my PTSD meant I felt anxious sitting inside. They understood that although sometimes I refused their offers of outings or company, I still wanted them to ask. They accepted that now it would always be them getting in touch and never me. They brought me thoughtful gifts and regularly sent check-in texts or emails to see how I was doing. They recognised that I might seem a bit more able to cope one day, only to crash down into the darkness the next. Above all, they showed me kindness, compassion and love as they listened to me talk about Harry and about my unending heartache. This is what my true friends did for me and I am so very grateful to them.

Unfortunately, as every bereaved person knows, or will soon discover, there are the friends who don't step up and who simply fail to be there for you. They might make the odd attempt to contact you but they don't try very hard, usually saying something insensitive like: 'Sorry I haven't been in touch, I've just been so busy!' Then there are others who mistakenly think you need space, especially if you don't respond to a text (probably because you're down the rabbit hole of incapacitating misery). That means they leave you alone, assuming you'll just be in touch when you're ready. I think most of us need to know that our friends are thinking of us and that they will remain persistent in keeping in touch until we feel able to take them up on an offer of a visit, taking us out or having a chat over FaceTime.

Worst of all, there are the friends who are silent. I haven't seen one of my oldest friends since Harry's funeral (I even chose her to read one of the poems). There are probably many reasons why friends abandon you at a time when you're experiencing the worst event that has ever happened to you. Presumably they find your grief uncomfortable or perhaps you're just not going to be fun to be with any more. Or maybe they don't have the compassion or empathy to imagine what it feels like to be in your shoes and, because your experience is just so alien to them, they back away and disappear from your life. These secondary losses feel so unjust, adding to the pain and heartbreak of a grief that is already more than enough to bear.

You may find you have fewer friends now, but aim to view it as a case of quality over quantity. I try to be as philosophical as I can about those who choose to stick with me through my darkest of times and those who don't. There is a saying – people come into your life for a reason, a season or a lifetime. Let go of the ones who were just here for a season and appreciate those who love you and stand steadfastly by you, the ones who are there for a reason or a lifetime.

Saying the Wrong Thing – or Saying Nothing

People in your life may occasionally say the wrong thing. Some may not fully grasp that you won't ever get over this and might say something like 'Time heals all wounds.' (In which case you could reply with this perceptive quote from Bob Geldof: 'Time doesn't heal; it accommodates.') They may talk about their children of a similar age, citing something trivial or annoying that their child has done, as they momentarily forget you can no longer do the same. All this can hurt. Overall, however, I feel that if people care about you and mean well, you have to just let it go.

I've found that it's people outside my inner circle (so acquaintances rather than friends) who are more inclined to say something clumsy or minimise your grief – and this can be upsetting. They may compare your loss to the death of their elderly parent or they may think 'OMG' is an appropriate response when sending you a message on hearing about the death of your child. Some may be insensitive enough to ask – as their first question – how they died. Regardless of the cause of death, this is incredibly intrusive, not to mention potentially extremely triggering. The best first question anyone (who hadn't previously known me) has asked so far is: 'What was he like?'

On the whole, though, grief makes a lot of people very uncomfortable. We're not very open about it in Western society and many people are terrified of speaking to a bereaved person, especially one who has lost a child. And yes, it's true, people will cross the road or pretend not to see you in order to avoid speaking to you. This may happen countless times. It's galling, but it says so much about them, not you. In the grand scheme of things and in light of what you're going through, they're just not worth wasting too much time over. As David Kessler says: 'What people think of your grief is none of your business.' Nevertheless, it hurts. A lot.

Most bereaved parents eventually learn to wear a mask because they soon realise that some people just aren't able to handle seeing someone who has experienced a traumatic loss. We are the living embodiment of their very biggest fear. We remind them that life is fragile and unpredictable; that it can end tragically. If it's happened to someone they know, it opens up the possibility that it could happen to them and that's frightening. Ultimately, they want to avoid having to confront these thoughts. We may even feel we need to 'protect' people from this in order to be able to interact with them and to function in the world. This may sadden or anger you, and rightly so. It's not right that those who are fortunate enough not to have gone through the extremity of pain that we have lack the compassion – or basic humanity – to acknowledge what it might be like for us. This reaction can make it feel as if losing a child is akin to having an infectious disease; it's as if people don't want to talk to you in case it's contagious.

There have now been many incidents when the death of my son has been the elephant in the room, unmentioned. And if I do bring the subject up myself in an attempt to dispel 'the elephant', I have found I may not get a response and what I've said is just ignored. Perhaps in addition to their own fears, people worry that mentioning our child will upset us – yet we want nothing more than to have them acknowledged and to speak openly about them. We need this as part of our healing and yet sometimes it's denied to us. It seems that speaking about the death of a child is taboo. Society's attitude towards mental health has changed enormously in recent years, so I very much hope it will eventually change towards bereavement, and child loss in particular, because it is just so wrong to be made to feel as if there is some sort of stigma around the death of your child. In the meantime, we should never feel we have to put on a brave face just to make others feel more comfortable. Equally, we should never feel we have to answer questions about the death of a loved one just to satisfy someone's curiosity. We have enough to deal with.

Compassion Fatigue

Although some people compound your pain, or simply fail to be there for you at all, there are those who thankfully stand by you and continue to do so. However, inevitably as time goes on, you will not be held in people's minds in the same way you were during the first agonising throes of bereavement. You may perhaps sense that, even though they care about you, they can't always face hearing about your ongoing pain. This is hard for the grieving person, who may still be struggling on a daily basis, but understandable for those around us for whom life goes on as normal. It isn't, after all, their loss. Sadly, this may mean that a few of those friends who were there for you in the beginning could eventually start to drift away. Although there are the much-appreciated brave few who remain loyally by your side, there is no doubt that the longer it is since your bereavement, the less frequently you may hear from some of your friends, and when they do check on you, the more you are expected to hold whole conversations without mentioning the one you've lost. Sometimes you can go along with this – and sometimes you can't.

Self-reliance

The reality is grief can feel horribly lonely. This is especially true as time goes on and a misguided assumption may be made by others that life will be getting easier – or even that you've got over your loss and are 'back to normal'. A lot of bereaved parents and widows/widowers report feeling very isolated because of this misconception. This is, without doubt, the most difficult of paths anyone has to walk in life. Whilst we can, of course, benefit enormously from the company of others, it may be worth considering whether this unique journey is one that we mainly have to make on our own. However, perhaps we don't actually need as much outside support as we initially think (whether from friends or a therapist/counsellor). If we can successfully look within, nurture our self-reliance and resilience and find our own path forward, we are less likely to feel let down and can potentially gain satisfaction from acquiring wisdom out of our suffering.

Pets

Sometimes the best therapist has fur and four legs.
Tiny Buddha

It has surprised me how much comfort our cats have given me. Neither of them is the type to curl up on your knee, unfortunately, but our older cat, as I have already said, nuzzles me when I'm upset and seems to sense Harry's presence (which the mediums confirmed). The younger cat serves a different purpose: his more boisterous energy provides light relief for us all. There is no doubt, they have both played a significant part in easing our grief at times, and I love that they now both live primarily in Harry's bedroom.

If our Compassionate Friends group is typical, then it seems very common to get a dog when you lose a child. Dogs provide a very positive purpose in that they get you up in the morning and you have to get out and take them for walks, plus they can be very affectionate. Pets are known to help with mental and emotional health and there's research to show that they can specifically reduce stress, anxiety, depression and loneliness and improve heart health, too.

Bereavement Groups

Although support groups aren't for everyone, they can provide comfort, connecting you with people who share your experience. This can mean you feel less lonely and isolated in your grief. I found our first Compassionate Friends meeting awe-inspiring: for the first time, I saw parents who had been through what we were going through, and who were functioning and coherent (at a point when I was neither). To see someone who shares your terrible loss but is further along the path can give you a sense of what your future might be like. There are those who act as beacons of light, bravely sharing how they navigate painful milestones such as birthdays, anniversaries, Christmas, as well as the difficulties of daily life. Life for these parents remains tough, but they are somehow coping. From the beginning, I looked to those members of our group who gave me hope that I would somehow survive, as they appeared to be doing.

Within this group that no one wants to have to belong to, everyone has the right to voice their viewpoint and have their individual experience of grief witnessed. I now see new members coming in, just as we once did, the pain of early grief etched on their faces, the sheer effort of coming in the first place all too evident. Most of us arrive knowing very few, if any, other bereaved parents, so we feel very alone in our harrowing experience. However, we soon learn that every one of us has suffered a terrible tragedy of the worst kind; sadly, we share a common bond.

There are Compassionate Friends groups all over the UK, as well as many other countries around the world. See the Appendix for details.

Chapter 6

Going Forward Without Those We Love

You can choose what you remember...
You can choose to carry hurt, pain, bitterness and anger.
You can choose to carry joy, love, laughter and light...
Let go of the hurt so there is room for love to grow.
Remember the life, not just the death...
Darcie D Sims

Sooner or later, it's up to us whether we remain in the depths of despair forever or do our best to gather together our own personal basket of resources, trying anything and everything to see if it might support us, even just a little. Actively engaging in our healing, whilst not in any way denying the stark truth of the loss that we have to carry, can lighten our burden as we travel through this new landscape that we now have to accept as our reality. David Kessler says that wounds will not heal in the darkness, they need to be aired and brought to the light. It's sometimes very tempting to remain in the darkness, but it's better if you use everything you possess to edge towards the light. This is, after all, surely what our loved ones would want for us. They would want us to look after ourselves and find as much joy and purpose as we can in our lives, despite their physical absence.

For me now, the purpose of life isn't to be happy. I think the possibility of happiness can feel torturously elusive to bereaved parents. From my new perspective, I see the true purpose of life as learning and evolving from my suffering, or at least doing my best to attempt to do so. If going forward there are moments of happiness along the way, then great, but when you have lost your child, your grief is inevitably a life sentence. However, I find it feels so much better to fill my heart with love for my son and live as much of a life as I'm able to. This is how I try to honour him.

I know only too well that there is no linear progress. I am very familiar now with the unnerving Snakes and Ladders grief game, but I am finding that it's now possible to have several 'better days' in a row. I no longer cry every single day, though I do still cry often. There are inevitably still some very dark days when the pain of my loss enfolds me once again, but I continue to strive towards improving my attempts to surf the waves of grief. Hope that it might get easier to bear my great loss is what propels me forward.

The fact is I can never go back to who I was or my old life and, unfortunately, I have no choice but to go forward in whatever way I can. I now have to live and grieve at the same time, hoping eventually to grieve with more love than pain, as they say. Human beings survive by adapting and evolving and I hope to use the fearless new part of me to do so, the part that no longer remotely fears death or what comes afterwards. Of course, in other ways, you live more fearfully when you have PTSD because the trauma causes a fear reaction that is excessively expressed. But for me at least, conversely, because the very worst has actually happened, I feel freed in some ways from a lot of the trivialities of life. The manifestation of your very worst fear can enable you to see everything from a very different perspective. Your mindset can shift in such a surprising way and the extremity of pain can create more depth in you, leading by contrast to more compassion and appreciation for the beautiful aspects of life. I hope, too, that I am wiser now.

Hope and Healing

When a child dies, a parent is still tied to that child.
Souls tied together across Universes.

It doesn't matter the age when they passed.
It doesn't matter how long ago it happened…their souls are forever tied.
That's the love of a parent.
That's the love that is more powerful than death…
Lexi Behrndt

They say the stronger the love, the harder the grief, and we know the love for a child is the strongest love of all. In the end, if we're going to survive, I believe there is no choice but to tether all that incredible limitless love we have and use it in all we go on to do without their physical presence. There is such a thing as a survivor mission, to make something good out of your tragedy. In my case, it's the desire to help through sharing my experiences and supporting others who are grieving.

Hope is paramount to my survival. In the early stages of grief, it may feel like you will never have hope again, but eventually, you do get to a point where it's safe to feel hopeful. Hope is about the future and it's sometimes more comfortable and familiar to stay in the past because that's where your loved one lived. But they can come into the future with you, because you can take them there with you, in your heart and memory, and if you believe in life after physical death, then you also know they're still with you anyway and this can definitely make life more bearable.

I feel enormous gratitude for Harry's short life, and I'm privileged to have been his mother. I was very fortunate to know him. I would prefer, going forward, for him to witness me navigating a way through somehow, rather than being forever tortured by my grief. Knowing me as he did, he would be aware of how hard it would be for me to survive this, but, if he is watching now, I imagine he would say: 'Come on Mum, you're doing really well, I'm so proud of you!'

Trauma therapist Michelle Rosenthal says that trauma creates change you don't choose but healing is about creating the change you do choose. I agree with this; I think healing is a choice. It's not an easy one and it's one I'm having to make over and over again. In all honesty, it's going to be a lifelong struggle living without Harry, but if I believe life has purpose and meaning, even if it's not always clear what this is, I hope I will be able to build a life around my devastation, as well as continuing my unbreakable bond with him. I will grieve forever and no doubt, sometimes, the darkness will continue to make me forget the light but, as Christina Rasmussen says, you can do the impossible because you've been through the unthinkable. I will have to use everything I've learnt to keep expanding and growing out of that darkness and to nurture the light.

I will live on, wrapping my boy tightly in my love and holding him in my heart until I can be with him again. I hope if you too have lost someone very precious, you eventually can do the same.

Epilogue

I know you're still with me...
but sometimes I wish I could reach into the sky and pull you to
my side.
Jane Lee Logan

Beyond the First Year

In Part One I wrote about whether the second year of bereavement might be better or worse than the first and, in truth, it's neither. It's different. One reason for this is that in my second year of grief, the world experienced – and is still experiencing as I write – a global pandemic. In the first year, my world was turned upside down and since then the actual world has been.

At the start of the pandemic, I was already very familiar with the loss of certainty and panic that I observed amongst non-grievers. In this particular respect, the rest of the world now had more in common with the bereaved. My life was already changed and restricted but suddenly, albeit for different reasons, everyone else found their lives to be changed and restricted too. However, it seems to me that the fear the virus instils in a lot of people has perhaps affected me less because my very worst fear has already been realised.

So, although Covid-19 in some respects hasn't made a huge difference to my life in the way it might have done for others, in other ways it has, adding an additional layer on top of my existing grief. I found it hard, during the first lockdown, not to meet up with the friends who supported me, and also because we couldn't go away – both of which had been essential for my survival during the first year.

Also challenging was hearing people say that they were 'grieving' for the life they used to lead, as was witnessing others behaving as if it was the end of the world when Christmas was effectively 'cancelled' in the UK; they were forgetting that, all being well, future Christmases would most likely go back to normal for them – this not being the case for those of us who have lost an irreplaceable family member. Whilst some may have equated the loss of their temporary freedom and cancelled plans with grief, it pales in comparison with the actual grief suffered by many as a result of the virus, or by those of us already coping with loss.

Aside from the pandemic, I have encountered my own serious health challenges during this time which subsequently triggered my PTSD once more. These health issues, I have no doubt, were caused by the severity of my trauma (and the doctor I saw agreed). I had thought, if I fully expressed my grief without suppression, I could avoid any health consequences resulting from the trauma. But perhaps my extreme physical responses to the shock caused more damage to my body at a cellular level than could ever possibly have been averted, despite my best efforts to counter them…

More positively, in the second year, I found that work helped quite a lot. I didn't need to worry about building up my practice again because I've been relatively busy despite Covid, holding consultations on Zoom. Work helps me for three reasons. One, it provides a distraction from my grief. I don't regret not starting back any sooner because I just wasn't ready, so the timing was right for me. Two, it provides some structure to my life. Having to put on a professional face can divert me from sliding down into a pit of despair and depression. And three, it helps me to help others. It gives me a purpose.

My views on life after death haven't changed. I have seen two more mediums, and had another reading with Claire Broad. They all imparted new information from Harry and, again, I felt bolstered by the indisputable evidence given that they couldn't possibly have had prior knowledge of. We have had fewer signs from Harry now, which I understand is common once they know you understand they're still around. But I continue to have conversations with him and I always feel him on my right side – in fact, I feel him as I write this. Sometimes he feels very close and sometimes he doesn't, and this is usually to do with how I feel, with how dense my grief is.

And I won't pretend – the pain of Harry's loss hasn't really lessened yet. Generally, life just seems to have flattened out beyond the first year. The shock has dissipated and I have now reached a certain resigned acceptance. I still cry a lot but it's different now, quieter, lonelier, less howling on my knees – though that does still happen once in a while. In hindsight, during the first year I was, perhaps understandably, impatient to be out of pain. From where I am now, I'm more accepting of that ongoing pain still being part of who I am at this point.

Yet, sometimes, the skies clear and I have a powerful sense of 'knowing' that's hard to describe. I feel Harry's energy and it seems increasingly purer and finer. Our communication feels progressively different from how it did when he was physically here. It appears that in our separation our connection somehow grows ever stronger, an invisible ethereal cord joining us together. When I align with this feeling of indestructible unconditional love, my heart and my soul seem to know something that my head doesn't – an indisputable knowing – and this brings me such peace, and even joy. Unfortunately, I struggle to remain in this state of being and my head wants to take control again. I get these glimpses and then I'm pulled back down into the realms of basic human emotions and suffering once more.

And although I generally function better on a daily basis, I still feel fragile and sometimes I continue to feel that I can't go on. I don't know when, or even if, this might get better. But I live in hope that it will. Hope is something I strive to hang on to – it's still all I have for my continued survival. I see how desperate I was to find hope in early grief – and I believe I was right to look for it and latch on to it when I felt able to. It kept me alive. It still does.

Recently, a bereaved mother told me how, five years on, she does now feel different, that it is better than it was in some ways, the grief less jagged around the edges. So, still, I hold on to hope and aspire to be like those that go ahead of me on this very difficult path, whilst endeavouring, as I go forward into the third year and beyond, to help those who follow behind.

Appendix

Reading

Recommended Books on Grief

Finding Meaning: The sixth stage of grief, David Kessler (Rider 2019)

Man's Search for Meaning, Viktor E Frankl (Rider 2004)

The Year of Magical Thinking, Joan Didion (Harper Perennial 2006)

Blue Nights, Joan Didion (Fourth Estate 2012)

Resilient Grieving: Finding strength and embracing life after a loss that changes everything, Lucy Hone PhD (The Experiment 2017)

It's OK That You're Not OK: Meeting grief and loss in a culture that doesn't understand, Megan Devine (Sounds True 2017)

When the Bough Breaks: Forever after the loss of a son or daughter, Judith R Bernstein PhD (Andrews McMeel Publishing 1998)

The Worst Loss: How families heal after the death of a child, Barbara D Rosof (Owl Books 1995)

The Unspeakable Loss: How do you live after a child dies? Nisha Zenoff PhD (Da Capo Lifelong Books 2017)

Beyond Tears: Living after losing a child, Ellen Mitchell (Griffin, 2009)

Caravan of No Despair: A memoir of loss and transformation, Mirabai Starr (Sounds True 2015)

Recommended Books for Exploring Life After Death

Life After Life, Raymond A Moody (Rider 2001)

Your Soul's Plan, Robert Schwartz (Frog Ltd 2009)

Your Soul's Gift, Robert Schwartz (Watkins Publishing 2013)

Permission to Mourn, Tom Zuba (Bish Press 2014)

Becoming Radiant, Tom Zuba (Bish Press 2018)

What the Dead Are Dying to Teach Us, Claire Broad (Watkins Publishing 2019)

Where Did You Go? A life-changing journey to connect with those we've lost, Christina Rasmussen (HarperOne 2020)

The Afterlife of Billy Fingers, Annie Kagan (Coronet 2014)

Answers from Heaven, Theresa Cheung and Claire Broad (Piatkus 2017)

My Son and the Afterlife, Elisa Medhus MD (Atria Books/Beyond Words 2015)

Start It Up, Rachel Pearson (HeartSign Press 2019)

Signs: The secret language of the universe, Laura Lynne Jackson (Piatkus 2019)

Recommended Films about Grief

Rabbit Hole (Nicole Kidman, Aaron Eckhart, Dianne Wiest) 2010

Collateral Beauty (Will Smith, Edward Norton, Kiera Knightley) 2016

Manchester by the Sea (Casey Affleck, Michelle Williams) 2016

Ordinary People (Donald Sutherland, Mary Tyler Moore, Timothy Hutton) 1980

Three Colours: Blue (Juliette Binoche) 1993

Podcasts for Grief

Shapes of Grief – a podcast by Liz Gleeson, bereavement therapist

Griefcast – a podcast hosted by comedian Caraid Lloyd

Key Organisations

This is primarily a UK-based list, though I have listed some organisations outside the UK, as in the cases of The Compassionate Friends and Helping Parents Heal.

All the mediums listed see clients from all over the world on Zoom.

If you are outside the UK, you should hopefully be able to find an equivalent organisation to those listed below.

The Compassionate Friends

The Compassionate Friends website is specifically for families who have lost a child of any age. They provide an incredible range of information, everything from advice on inquests to loss through murder or suicide, plus retreats and a helpline run by bereaved parents. I found all their individual sections enormously helpful (there's nothing they haven't covered) and can't emphasise enough how much of a lifeline this organisation was for me in early grief.

- https://www.tcf.org.uk/
- For siblings: https://www.tcf.org.uk/content/ftb-siblings/
- For grandparents: https://www.tcf.org.uk/content/ftb-grandparents/

Outside the UK:

- US: https://www.compassionatefriends.org/
- Canada: http://tcfcanada.net/
- Australia: https://tcfa.org.au/

Cruse Bereavement Care

Cruse is the UK's largest bereavement charity, providing advice and information on support groups and bereavement counselling to people suffering from grief of all kinds. They have a free helpline.

- https://www.cruse.org.uk/

The Good Grief Trust

An alternative umbrella organisation to Cruse that is rapidly growing, again covering all types of grief. The Good Grief Guide is run by the bereaved, for the bereaved. They're very active on social media and say they aim to be the UK's leading fully comprehensive online bereavement service, bringing bereavement into the twenty-first century and changing the perception of grief in British society.

- https://www.thegoodgrieftrust.org/

The Coroners' Courts Support Service

The Coroners' Courts Support Service provides volunteers who will come with you to an inquest, talk you through the process on the day and just generally provide kindness and support. We had one of these volunteers and I'm pleased we did. There is also a helpline and lots of links to information on their website to help you understand the inquest process which can be so very daunting:

- https://coronerscourtssupportservice.org.uk/

They also have a page that has useful links to organisations which specialise in various types of unexpected death, such as drugs or alcohol, road accidents, stillbirths and so on:

- https://coronerscourtssupportservice.org.uk/useful-links-organisations/

Sudden

This organisation provides information specifically on coping with a sudden bereavement. There's a page specifically related to losing a child suddenly, with links to more specific help, depending on how they died. There is also a helpline.

- https://www.sudden.org/

At A Loss

A signposting website, directing the bereaved to the most appropriate services. There is a section specifically for people aged 18 to 30 who have been bereaved and a section for men (who sometimes don't seek support or talk through their grief in the way women do). There is also a counsellor live chat service.

- https://www.ataloss.org/

Where to get help if you feel suicidal:

As previously mentioned, suicidal ideation is not unusual if your child has died. However, if necessary, I urge you to please seek help or use the following helpline.

The Samaritans:

- www.samaritans.org
- Call: 116 123

Resources for Grief Support

Nutritional Therapy

Nutritional Therapy can help with some of the physical symptoms that occur with grief and trauma. Look for a registered nutritional therapist with a degree-level qualification in nutritional medicine.

The British Association for Nutrition and Lifestyle Medicine (BANT):

- https://bant.org.uk/

Vanessa May, BANT-registered nutritional therapist:

- https://www.wellbeingandnutrition.co.uk/

Bereavement Counselling

Your GP may be able to refer you to a local service, though there can be long waiting lists in some areas. Cruse and the Good Grief Trust can provide information on bereavement counsellors or therapists in your area.

- Cruse: https://www.cruse.org.uk/
- The Good Grief Trust: https://www.thegoodgrieftrust.org/

Holistic Grief Coaching

Grief coaching can be a valid alternative to traditional bereavement counselling. Currently it is more prevalent in the USA than in the UK. My version of grief coaching is holistic, addressing the effects grief can have on the mind, body and spirit. I understand completely the far-reaching consequences of losing a child in a way that most therapists may not be able to. Talking to someone who has actually experienced your pain can make all the difference, though I always acknowledge too that everyone has their own unique experience. I can give you a safe space to express and process your grief, as well as provide professional advice on both the physical and emotional impact, suggesting tools and strategies you can use to ease this very difficult journey.

I work with clients from the UK and elsewhere in the world over Zoom.

- https://www.wellbeingandnutrition.co.uk

Support Groups

Support groups aren't for everyone – and I never thought they'd be for me – but they can be a lifeline, especially in the case of child loss when you are unlikely to know many, if any, people who share your experience. I recommend at least trying your local Compassionate Friends to see if it could be a potential means of support for you.

- The Compassionate Friends: https://www.tcf.org.uk/

Outside the UK:

- US: https://www.compassionatefriends.org/
- Canada: http://tcfcanada.net/
- Australia: https://tcfa.org.au/

Other organisations that provide information on support groups for grief of all kinds:

- Cruse: https://www.cruse.org.uk/
- The Good Grief Trust: https://www.thegoodgrieftrust.org/

Yoga for Grief

I highly recommend Yoga with Adriene. This gentle online 25-minute class is perfect for early grief when you might not want to leave the house to attend a class. However, I still find it benefits me beyond the first year.

- https://yogawithadriene.com/yoga-for-grief/

Reiki

This form of energy healing can potentially help you feel a little more relaxed and balanced. You can find a practitioner here:

- https://www.reikifed.co.uk/

EMDR

EMDR stands for Eye Movement Desensitisation and Reprocessing and is a form of therapy specifically for trauma. You may be able to ask your GP for a referral. Otherwise, you can find out more and search for a practitioner in your area here:

- https://emdrassociation.org.uk/

EFT

Emotional Freedom Technique (EFT) can be done face to face or online. You can search for a practitioner here:

- https://www.findatherapy.org/emotional-freedom-technique

Mediums

- Claire Broad: http://www.clairevoyant.co.uk/
- Kathy Busby: https://www.pathwaystospirit.com/

- Julie Soskin: https://www.juliesoskin.com/
- Isabella Johnson: https://thesoulreadingmedium.com/

Helping Parents Heal

Helping Parents Heal is a non-profit organisation dedicated to providing support and resources to aid in the healing process. They go a step beyond other groups by allowing the open discussion of spiritual experiences and evidence for the afterlife, in a non-dogmatic way. There are Helping Parents Heal branches and Facebook groups all over the world – see the main USA website to find a branch in your area:

- https://www.helpingparentsheal.org/ (USA website)
- Facebook page for the UK: Helping Parents Heal UK

About the Author

Vanessa May lives in London with her husband, daughter and two cats. She is a nutritional therapist and wellbeing coach and now also offers a unique type of bereavement support.

Vanessa's holistic grief coaching looks at all aspects of the grieving process and how it can affect not only our emotional and mental wellbeing but also the body and the spirit. Vanessa's expansion into supporting others who are grieving evolved from not being able to find the help she needed when her son died and from having to determine her own ways to navigate a complex grieving process. Vanessa's experience means she is able to guide others who are going through what she has been through with heartfelt compassion, as well as being in a position to provide professional advice.

She hopes to shine a light through the darkness of grief for other bereaved families.

To find out more about working with Vanessa:

- www.wellbeingandnutrition.co.uk
- email: vanessa@wellbeingandnutrition.co.uk
- Instagram: @may.wellbeing
- Twitter: @maywellbeing
- Facebook: Wellbeing and Nutrition

Author website:
- www.vanessamay.co.uk

Other books by Vanessa May:

- *Supporting Your Grieving Client: A guide for wellness practitioners* (to be published July 2023 by Singing Dragon)

Know you're being guided, by all of us who have survived this impossible hell.
You may not hear us, or see us, but we are with you.
Beside you.
Hand in hand, heart to heart.
Always.
Just like your child still is...
Angela Miller, *A Bed for My Heart*

Acknowledgements

With much love to my family who walk this difficult path with me.

To the friends who have loyally stood by me and consistently offer their love and support.

A special mention to Jessica (who kindly read multiple drafts), Bronwen, Elaine – and not forgetting Anthony – who all read my early drafts and who encouraged me and believed in my ability to write.

Many thanks as well to the incredible author Nancy Tucker for her sensitive editing and encouragement.

Also, to Enda Kenneally for his editing and support, and for his unwavering belief in this book.

And lastly, thank you to my beautiful boy Harry, my adored son whose light guides me forward, whose presence I feel daily and who I continue to love unconditionally and for all eternity.

AYNI
BOOKS

ALTERNATIVE HEALTH & HEALING

"Ayni" is a Quechua word meaning "reciprocity" - sharing, giving
and receiving - whatever you give out comes back to you. To
be in Ayni is to be in balance, harmony and right relationship
with oneself and nature, of which we are all an intrinsic part.
Complementary and Alternative approaches to health and wellbeing essentially follow a holistic model, within which one is given
support and encouragement to move towards a state of balance,
true health and wholeness, ultimately leading to the awareness of
one's unique place in the Universal jigsaw of life - Ayni, in fact.
If you have enjoyed this book, why not tell other readers by
posting a review on your preferred book site.

Recent bestsellers from AYNI Books are:

Reclaiming Yourself from Binge Eating
A Step-By-Step Guide to Healing
Leora Fulvio, MFT
Win the war against binge eating, wake up each morning at peace
with your body, unafraid of food and overeating.
Paperback: 978-1-78099-680-6 ebook: 978-1-78099-681-3

The Reiki Sourcebook (revised ed.)
Frans Stiene, Bronwen Stiene
A popular, comprehensive and updated manual for the Reiki
novice, teacher and general reader.
Paperback: 978-1-84694-181-8 ebook: 978-1-84694-648-6

The Chakras Made Easy
Hilary H. Carter
From the successful Made Easy series, Chakras Made Easy is a
practical guide to healing the seven chakras.
Paperback: 978-1-78099-515-1 ebook: 978-1-78099-516-8

The Inner Heart of Reiki
Rediscovering Your True Self
Frans Stiene
A unique journey into the inner heart of the system of Reiki, to
help practitioners and teachers rediscover their True Selves.
Paperback: 978-1-78535-055-9 ebook: 978-1-78535-056-6

Middle Age Beauty
Soulful Secrets from a Former Face Model Living Botox Free in her
Forties
Machel Shull
Find out how to look fabulous during middle age without plastic
surgery by learning inside secrets from a former model.
Paperback: 978-1-78099-574-8 ebook: 978-1-78099-575-5

The Optimized Woman
Using Your Menstrual Cycle to Achieve Success and Fulfillment
Miranda Gray
If you want to get ahead, get a cycle! For women who want to
create life-success in a female way.
Paperback: 978-1-84694-198-6

The Patient in Room Nine Says He's God
Louis Profeta
A roller coaster ride of joy, controversy, triumph and tragedy;
often all on the same page.
Paperback: 978-1-84694-354-6 ebook: 978-1-78099-736-0

Re-humanizing Medicine
A Holistic Framework for Transforming Your Self, Your Practice,
and the Culture of Medicine
David Raymond Kopacz
Re-humanizing medical practice for doctors, clinicians, clients, and
systems.
Paperback: 978-1-78279-075-4 ebook: 978-1-78279-074-7

**You Can Beat Lung Cancer Using Alternative/Integrative
Interventions**
Carl O. Helvie R.N., Dr.P.H.
Significantly increase your chances of long-term lung cancer
survival by using holistic alternative and integrative interventions
by physicians or health practitioners.
Paperback: 978-1-78099-283-9 ebook: 978-1-78099-284-6

Readers of ebooks can buy or view any of these bestsellers by
clicking on the live link in the title. Most titles are published in
paperback and as an ebook. Paperbacks are available in traditional
bookshops. Both print and ebook formats are available online.

Find more titles and sign up to our readers' newsletter at http://
www.johnhuntpublishing.com/mind-body-spirit
Follow us on Facebook at https://www.facebook.com/OBooks and
Twitter at https://twitter.com/obooks